WHAT A
SON
NEEDS FROM
HIS DAD

WHAT A
SON
NEEDS
FROM
HIS DAD

HOW A MAN PREPARES HIS SONS FOR LIFE

MICHAEL A. O'DONNELL, PhD

BETHANYHOUSE
a division of Baker Publishing Group
Minneapolis, Minnesota

© 1996, 2011 by Michael O'Donnell

Previously published as *How a Man Prepares His Sons for Life*

Published by Bethany House Publishers
11400 Hampshire Avenue South
Bloomington, Minnesota 55438
www.bethanyhouse.com

Bethany House Publishers is a division of
Baker Publishing Group, Grand Rapids, Michigan

Printed in the United States of America

ISBN: 978-0-7642-3190-2

Unless otherwise identified, Scripture quotations are from the Holy Bible, New International Version®. NIV®. Copyright © 1973, 1978, 1984 by Biblica, Inc.™ Used by permission of Zondervan. All rights reserved worldwide. www.zondervan.com

Scripture quotations identified KJV are from the King James Version of the Bible.

Cover design by Rob Williams, InsideOutCreativeArts

18   19   20   21   22   23   24   7   6   5   4   3   2   1

To my son, Patrick—who has become *all* that I had ever hoped and prayed for in a godly man.

Ad Majorem Dei Gloriam

Contents

Acknowledgments

To my wife, Rachel, my consultant-in-residence, who is always there for me with a new thought, a better phrase, and a word of blessing and encouragement—I love you!

To my daughter, Kayla, who is a superb writer and illustrator—I dig that about you!

To my son, Patrick: You made me want to be a better dad.

To my twin brother and best friend, Richard: Thanks for all that you do for me—which is too much to put in print!

To my older brother, Billy, whose love and concern for my welfare is the reason I'm still alive today.

To the good folks of St. Matthias Episcopal Church and Father Scott Campbell, Rector: I love you with the love of the Lord.

Preface

When I was a young dad, one day I found myself listening to the way my son talked. I began to hear more of his mother's warm, witty, and very personable manner of speech. Patrick already had many of my wife's physical features, but I guess I hadn't thought about how truly verbal he was.

Rachel is an excellent talker, too. Although I'm known for my skills behind a lectern or pulpit, it's really my wife who can turn a phrase. Many times I've wanted to record her speaking, because it's more than *what* she says, it's *how* she says it that really holds my attention.

There I was in my son's room. It was late and I was getting ready to put him to bed. Patrick was looking at me, telling me a story in just the same way Rachel would. The same mannerisms. The same facial expressions. The same tone of voice.

I thought to myself, *How does he copy her so well? Is it in the genes or is it some environmental thing?*

Just then Rachel came into the bedroom and said to Patrick, "Okay, guy, it's time for bed. Kiss Daddy good-night and get under the covers. I'll be in to read to you from *The Chronicles of Narnia*."

Then it hit me. Of course, she read to him! It was their bedtime ritual. And so, on a regular basis—whether Patrick was consciously aware of it or not—he was taking in *every* word. *Every* idea. Every night. But just as important, he was capturing her style and personality. Not just what she said but how she said it. Why, he was imitating her—hook, line, and sinker! I thought to myself, *This is good.*

The Bible says we should keep in mind those who have spoken the Word of God to us and consider their manner or way of life and imitate it (see Hebrews 13:7). It also says that God's Son is the express image of himself (see Hebrews 1:3). And now, before me, I have a son who—when telling a dramatic story—is the exact representation of his mother.

My point is this: As we prepare our sons for life, our job is as simple as it is challenging. At its most basic level, our job as fathers involves living in a way that makes a lasting impression on our sons, so that our best ways become their ways.

As I was watching Patrick get ready for bed, I noticed that he had *my* habit of talking too quickly. We called it "fast talk." And sometimes he ran his thoughts together at such high speed that I couldn't comprehend a single word. Yes, he copied the good as well as the not so good!

Some of you may remember the public service announcement that ran on TV during the '70s. In it we saw a little boy walking with his dad. The dad picks up a stone and throws it; the son picks up a stone and throws it. The dad washes his car with a hose; the son washes his car with a water pistol. The dad takes a pack of cigarettes out of his top pocket and, lighting one up, begins to smoke. The son reaches for the pack of cigarettes the father has laid on the ground, and the voice-over says, "Like father, like son—think about it."

Very convincing. So much so that media experts tell us that cigarette purchases by men dropped significantly during the years that particular PSA ran. Now, that's the power of TV—and it's the power of fatherhood.

Even so, we fathers forget that we are being watched. Studied, if you please, to see how things are done. When children are young, they want so much to be like us. Do the things we do. Watch the same TV programs. See the same movies. Have the same heroes. Root for the same athletic teams. Wear the same clothes!

So much so that years ago, Madison Avenue came out with father-and-son wear. A kid could put on the same designer clothing as dear ol' dad. Like conjoined twins, they could even sport the same underwear—indistinguishable in color and style. No doubt this is great stuff. I only wish raising my son right had been as easy as dressing alike! But you and I know it isn't that easy.

That night when Rachel came back into Patrick's bedroom and I wandered out of it, I thought, *What kind of impact am I going to make on him? What will I have passed on to him when he walks out that door one day . . . all grown up, headed for college or his first job away from home? Maybe with a girl on his arm and marriage on his mind? What will I have taught him about life, love, work?* I've had some pretty intense experiences on the job, like the time I worked for a guy who kept trying to test me to see if I'd go along with something immoral or unethical. I don't know what his problem was, but it really got to me because he was supposed to be a Christian. Would Patrick be ready to work for some demon-boss? What about when so-called buddies came along, offering a joint to smoke? Or a girl who would love to make him feel *really* nice?

We've got to be there for our sons. The world is impacting them and calling to them all the time. The day they leave home will be the moment of truth. Will they be ready to stand on their own two feet? Will they have sufficient moral courage to do what is right? Will they acknowledge God in all of their ways—in marriage, in home life, and on the job? The answers to these questions will be greatly affected by our intentional involvement in their lives now . . . or our lack of involvement. With nothing left to chance, we can begin to influence, shape, and guide them—helping to mold them into young men of strength and integrity.

In the following pages is my sincere effort to enter into a dialogue with you. I care deeply about the potential impact of such a book on your life, so much so that I asked men from all over America to pray for me as I wrote. I asked them to pray for God's guidance, because I know beyond any doubt that God wants each one of us to learn what a son needs from his dad.

Therefore, may God richly bless you as you read. Most important, may He help you to prepare your sons for life— "on earth as it is in heaven" (Matthew 6:10).

1

Before Your Son Faces
the World

The Beatles were back! The "fab three" were talking about their reunion that took twenty-five years to pull off. In one interview[1] with Paul McCartney, Paul talks about years earlier having played cowboys and Indians with John Lennon's son, Julian. After all the "bang-bang, you're dead" stuff, Lennon pulled McCartney over and asked, "How do you do that?" John was uncomfortable with his own son. "I couldn't tell him," Paul confesses. "You either know how to do that stuff or you don't."

Paul McCartney is right. So much of what we do as adults we learned watching our own parents when we were kids. That's why creating a good father-son relationship is so important. From the interview with Paul McCartney, we learn that his upbringing made him "comfortable with children." His father rolled on the ground with him, took him hiking through the woods, and—you bet!—played cowboys and

Indians with him. As the saying goes, "One good father is worth a hundred schoolmasters." Now grown and with children of his own, Paul McCartney *knows how it's done.*

The Bible says it best: "Train a child in the way he should go, and when he is old he will not turn from it" (Proverbs 22:6). The problem is, when citing this proverb, we usually highlight only the positive applications of the verse—like Paul McCartney being played with as a child and now as an adult playing with his own children. But what about John Lennon? We need to keep in mind that some kinds of training can have a negative effect, as well.

Consider the generational effects of alcoholism. A man can have the tendencies of an alcoholic even though he's never taken a drop of alcohol into his mouth. How is that possible? If he was raised in a home where one or both parents were alcoholic—or even raised by the children of alcoholics—it's possible he could have, as an adult, the psychological and emotional makeup of an alcoholic. He could be a compulsive gambler, for example. He could find it hard to hold down a job, or find it difficult to maintain intimacy with his wife. This is the negative application of the proverb: Train up a child *in the emotional and behavioral ways of an alcoholic,* and when he is older he will not turn *or depart from being an alcoholic.*

That's why the role of a father preparing his sons for life is so important. We need to understand the dangers of a do-as-I-say-but-not-as-I-do style of fathering. We also need to consider the rewards of a job well done. One father told me that the greatest joy he'd ever known came the day his oldest son called to say thanks for always being there to give direction about any decision he faced, big or small.

How do we intentionally, deliberately, consistently, and adequately prepare our sons for life? Maybe you've seen the startling statistics. We know about the sons who have run amuck. We see young men all around us who are crumbling and caving in to drugs, illicit sexual relationships, homosexuality, and bisexuality. We see young men who don't know how to accept direction or respond appropriately to authority. We wonder, *How will my son make it in life? In his work? In his marriage? Will he be a strong Christian or a church dropout? Will he be a careless spender or a financial success?*

If we're honest, we know that most men who blow it fall apart in one major area of their life. Maybe it's a secret attraction to pornography, gambling that gets out of hand, or a bad temper. Whatever it is, it's that one fatal flaw that goes unchecked or underestimated that eventually pulls a man down.

The challenge of preparing a son to be a man of responsibility and integrity is great. There are seven core issues that every father can work on with his son to lay a foundation of healthy masculine character. They are preparing our sons to be:

1. devout disciples of Christ;
2. good citizens;
3. holders of worthy vocations; responsible workers;
4. choosers of good friends;
5. able to enjoy life;
6. sexually chaste; understanding of male sexuality; avoiding the hazards of pornography; and
7. lovers of their wives; supporters of their marriages.

Now, before we begin to explore each of these areas, you and I need to pray—for apart from the Lord we can do nothing (see John 15:5). Some of us only pay lip service to God, running to Him only after trouble strikes. This, of course, is a symptom of our male self-sufficiency. We need to realize before all else that our success as fathers will depend on our relationship with God.

The good news is that God does not leave you or me on our own. Because your son is a gift from the Lord (see Psalm 127:3), God intended you, and no one else, to train him up! He gave you special resources—His Word, prayer, and the Holy Spirit, to name a few—to aid you in your parenting task. Therefore, in prayer, ask Him to hold you accountable to accept the challenge, the commitment. You, unlike any other person on the face of the earth, stand in a strategic position to prepare your son to become a man of strength and character. Ask Him to reveal any "family histories" that need to be broken. Ask Him to help you to be honest about your heart motives and dreams for your son.

David Simmons, author of *Dad the Family Coach*, calls this special provision from God "father power." And alluding to a father's influence as found in Exodus 34:7, he concludes:

> God wants His truth and light to pass from one generation to another, so He established an automatic device to fit into the family to insure His wishes. He created father power with the strength to span four generations and inserted it into the hearts of fathers. Father power is like a tool, a claw hammer, to extract the truth about God out of one generation and pound it into the next generation, and the third and the fourth. [2]

But father power given by God will be unused or misused unless we hook up to the right source. Our father power is not our anger, our money, or our ability to chill out and let nothing our sons do bother us. Instead, it's our call to rely on God to help us instill in our sons certain core principles and values. We are called to raise sons in the nurture and counsel of the Lord. That means active love and active training—both in equal amounts!

We're not talking about raising perfect sons or holier-than-thou plaster saints. We are talking about raising balanced, healthy young men who have a strong inner core, who are not emotionally crippled and unable to love and lead their families. Sons who can take center stage in the world—in business, in church, in the community—and be confident in their God-given abilities.

You and I want to give our sons good ground to stand on, strength to "take the field" when their time comes. We men know the temptations that are out there—the opportunities to cheat; to power-broker and bully; to pursue escapes like drugs or alcohol; to have illicit sex; or simply to cave in to life's pressures.

With the help of God, we can be the mentors our sons need. With His guidance and the help of other strong Christian men, we can prepare our sons to be true champions for God—men who do not sacrifice their bodies, their hearts, their minds, and their souls to a world of unhealthy compromises. We can prepare them to take the right turns in the road, to heed good advice, and to build their lives upon sound biblical principles. Our preparation can help them reach the highest limits of their masculine strengths. As we explore the ways in which we can mentor our sons, let's commit to pray every day for God to lead and guide us in this most wonderful and noble task *of giving our sons what they need from us!*

For Thought and Discussion

1. What kind of father power do you use? Is it your anger, your money, your strength? Focus on the task of mentoring: training your son, preparing him for life. How is that task a powerful one?

2. What areas of your son's life do you have a tendency to neglect, letting someone else do it for you? Are they areas you feel incompetent in yourself (e.g., math, computers, sports)? Discuss pros and cons of abdicating our mentoring role in some cases.

2

Effective Fathering

Larry sits in my office. His hands tightly clenched. His right foot nervously tapping the floor. He has anxiety written all over his face. He has come to talk about his father, whom he calls "The Invisible Dad." An unwelcome tear surfaces and he wipes it away fiercely. "He was never there for me," Larry says softly. Then comes a halting, deep breath. He asks, dead serious, "Do you think he knows just how much leaving me on my own has screwed up my life?"

Larry started having sex when he was fourteen. His luck, he confesses, ran out when he was sixteen and got his girlfriend pregnant. She had an abortion. Later they had a fight, and he split. Larry also has problems holding down even a part-time job. "I've never had a boss I didn't hate," Larry says with a deep-throated chuckle. Then he catches himself. I am his professor. He throws a sheepish look my way, and the laughter subsides.

Larry is one of my freshmen. No matter how much I try to bolster him, his self-esteem remains fragile. Outwardly, at university, he comes across cool and collected and thoroughly at ease in the company of his peers. But a colleague tells me that Larry has talked about wanting to kill himself. The issue of his father—a relationship shaped by silence and emotional distance—seems critical to understanding his musings about suicide. I have invited Larry into my office to talk to him. When I ask about his father, this normally joking, defiant young man becomes a little boy. His mood darkens. He is weak and insecure. He shares only fragmented negative glimpses into the world of his deadbeat parent. I view him as a man who thought giving his son food, clothes, and a roof over his head was good enough.

Larry represented a growing number of young men I saw in my office on a daily basis. Adolescents whose fathers chose to disconnect from their families because they were too preoccupied with their work or other pursuits. We are not talking about poor, uneducated fathers. We are talking about men from the whole spectrum of society, whose "absence" is creating devastating consequences. Consider two of our nation's most pressing problems—crime and teenage pregnancy. Researchers now demonstrate that the most reliable predictor of these behaviors has nothing to do with race or income. It is the family structure. Pregnant and delinquent teens come from fatherless homes. That's why talking about this right up front is so important.

As fathers who want to give our sons what they need, you and I must understand the full range of our fathering responsibilities. Fatherhood is more than bringing home a paycheck. It is more than the curiously old-fashioned idea of being the disciplinarian of the home. Most would reject out-of-hand the "animal" view of fathering: "Any male can father a baby." But do we question the more subtle images of manhood being passed off these days? The man who is more a *banker,* a *body builder,* a *computer wizard,* or *escape artist* than a man? You and I want the most effective model, not one created in the image of our fallen nature.

Take a look at some dads who are out-of-balance. Certain aspects of their training may be good, but they are not fully adequate.

The Military Dad

Christopher Plummer, as Captain von Trapp in *The Sound of Music,* plays the typical military dad to a T—whistling a series of signals to his children to have them assemble downstairs, line up in descending order by age, and stand at attention. "Just make 'em obey" is his parenting philosophy. "Children are to be seen and not heard" is his creed. This style says fathering consists of a list of rules to be blindly followed. Commands are to be obeyed, period. In his home, Captain von Trapp is the company commander, and his tykes are the foot soldiers he leads into battle against disorder and delay.

Christopher Plummer played this part in a way that was charming and benign. The real-life "military dad" is hard, and the effect of his demanding, disapproving style is damaging. He may never have been in the military, but he sure knows how to bark orders and instill fear.

Shepherd Bliss, a young husband and father of three, knows the routine all too well. In an interview in the *Los Angeles Times Magazine*[1] on fathers and sons, he recalls growing up in a military family, the child and grandson of army officers. At the dinner table, Shepherd recalls how his family ate in silence. "Lifting our forks to our mouths as though performing some military exercise," explained Shepherd, "we'd all trace a right angle in the air."

His father was domineering and sometimes violent, acting more like a drill sergeant than a dad. Now a Berkeley psychologist, Bliss, fifty-one, says of his military father: "I think it's one of my deepest problems, a lack of that father-son connection. . . . I am in rebellion against traditional masculinity." Is it any surprise that, in direct opposition to his father's views, he led an anti-war movement inside the military while serving as an army officer during the Vietnam War? The military, he says, was happy to let him go!

Of course not every man in the service will live out this flawed view of fathering. Any man can resort to rigid discipline and hard pressure. The problem with the military approach to fathering is that it uses force—emotional, psychological, and even physical manipulation—in an attempt to exert control. This kind of dad uses physical punishment or verbal assaults that might include put-downs, shouting, ridicule, and sarcasm. He withholds love and approval by giving his son the cold shoulder. . . . Tally this up and you may create a son who is a tough guy on the outside but suffering from angry turmoil, depression, and low self-esteem on the inside.

The Hypocrite Dad

This is the do-as-I-say-but-not-as-I-do kind of guy. In this household, Dad is often seen by his children as hypocritical because his Christian witness is limited to Sunday morning. During the week he doesn't quite practice what he preaches—at home or at work.

"I saw my father as a hypocrite," says Bill. He hesitates for a moment because of the knot that twists in his stomach as he remembers, but continues, "We were Catholic and attended Mass every Sunday. [My father] would pray piously, listen to sermons about social justice, take Communion, and return home unchanged. He would curse relatives privately, charm them in person, and curse them again, all in a day. On weekends, if someone from his office called, I had to lie and say he wasn't home. . . . I lay awake at night, listening through the thin wall of our suburban home as he yelled at my mother. I lay very still, as if by stillness I could quiet the storm."[2]

The dangers of being a hypocrite are obvious if we're asking our sons to lie or cheat. But there is another, more subtle scenario—one that will perhaps strike closer to home.

I can remember Sunday mornings as the most turbulent and chaotic day of the week. It would begin early as one of my parents would pound on the bathroom door, screaming at me to get out and let my sister get in. Then it was downstairs for breakfast where Tom, my younger brother, and I would fight over cereal boxes to read while we ate our Cheerios or Wheaties. This caused my dad, half-dressed, to burst out of his bedroom to separate us, sometimes even spank us.

Next came the car ride to church and the inevitable refereeing by Dad: "Stop hitting your sister!" "Will you move over and quit picking on your brother!" And of course the ultimate threat, "Stop or I'll pull the car over!"

After all this fighting we'd arrive at the church parking lot, and my parents would turn to us and say, "Okay, everyone smile now." And we would. Big grins, too! Like actors walking on stage. Reciting our lines, we'd say something like "Good morning! Isn't it just great to be in church?"

But we kids didn't buy it—not for a minute. Dad wasn't a bad guy, you understand. But we knew the truth that lay just beneath the surface. To be heavenly at church meant going through hell at home. We also knew that Sunday was the time to look good and be on our best behavior. Our hair was combed, our shoes shined, our Bibles in hand. We did our part to help the family maintain its facade of whitewashed spirituality.

My dad was not a hypocrite. He was a normal, stressed-out guy, trying to get his family cleaned up for church. The problem is that when I became a teenager, it was hard to take the faith of my father seriously. Was religion only a way to make other people think well of you? A front? My religion seemed shallow and full of flaws. And yet I desired a real faith, with real prayers and a real relationship with God. But I didn't know if it really existed, if it was really possible to attain.

Hypocrite dads can cause their sons to disassociate from anything worthwhile, suspecting that goodness and virtue are all a fraud. I saw this at times with my students—particularly male students. For example, when it came time to go to chapel and listen to a guest speaker, many tuned him or her out—believing that much of what they had to say wasn't true anyway. Even with collegiate fund-raisers, many were largely unmotivated to give or to get others to give.

When they were asked why, some said things like, "Most of the money will be misused" or "It may be embezzled." Such cynicism is strange to hear, considering the university where I taught has a positive reputation. But it does highlight how older children today are more suspicious of adults and mistrusting of their claims after years of watching them fail to practice what they preach.

The Business Partner Dad

The father of a student in the movie *Dead Poets Society* depicts the business partner dad perfectly. He's the guy who cares only about his son's professional grooming. So much so that, in this particular case, he refuses to acknowledge his son's acting ability. And believing that drama will not further the boy's professional career goals, he even goes so far as to forbid his son to be involved in a dramatic presentation being performed by his preparatory school.

In one particularly cruel scene, the father takes on the boy in a verbal tongue-lashing—belittling his son's aspirations to become an actor. "That's not why I've sent you to school!" the father shouts. "You're going to Harvard to be a medical doctor . . . to do the things I never got to do." The son is devastated that his future is not his own and, in the early hours of a Sunday morning, the father discovers that his only child—bright, and blessed with a promising future— has committed suicide.

An extreme example, maybe, but the business partner dad is interested in the material side of life. He talks of his son's prosperity in monetary terms. Spirituality—as a concept or practice—is either vague or a non-issue. His son's soul and faith development may be virtually ignored; at least they take a backseat to success and "getting ahead." Attending church may be a good thing to do—it's part of the grooming—but never to be taken very seriously. The things that matter to this dad are attending the "right" schools, having the "right" friends, and saying the "right" things. No leap in the logic here: A man simply gets what he deserves—the old-fashioned way—he earns it!

True, some business partner dads only want to train their sons to get a jump-start on other kids coming out of high school or college, maybe even preparing them to survive the hard knocks of a competitive world. This is understandable.

But too often a son can begin to believe that achievement is how to merit Dad's favor. Every success at school or at work gives him a reason to love me. Fail, and the consequences include being ignored or feeling Dad's huge disappointment. This kind of pass-fail system can transfer over to a boy's perceptions of God. God only loves me when I do what He wants. And so God's love, like Dad's, is conditional. This can cause a boy to be largely indifferent to spiritual things.

The Super Spiritual Dad

This guy is almost the opposite of the business partner dad. Where the former focuses too much on things material, this guy concentrates only on the spiritual or religious side of life. To him, everything can be broken down into two categories—the sacred and the profane. Being a man looks like this: Just learn the Bible; the only worthy ambition in life is to be a pastor or missionary. Never mind that your son is gifted in science or baseball.

Boys who are raised by super spiritual dads sometimes complain that their interests apart from Bible study are ignored and that their father's religious interests are pushed on them. Sports, art, music, money, and entrepreneurialism get little encouragement. Sometimes the dad is a real legalist, and the world is viewed in very limited, black-and-white terms. Children feel that their freedom to pursue hobbies, read classical literature, do mathematics, play with computers, or mix with "unsaved" kids is severely limited or entirely prohibited.

This dad may think, *Forming my son's character and training him has to be done away from "secular" people who will be a bad influence on him. Nothing secular should ever be permitted to shape my boy's outlook.*

There is some element of truth here. Certainly the world's influences through print media, radio, TV, and computers should be scrutinized. Yes, we should be strong enough to ban "trash TV" and harmful music. But our sons need not be raised in a religious "hothouse" to keep them "safe" from the world. Many kids raised in highly spiritual environments go off to Christian colleges and still get into trouble. Why?

Because commitment to God is a matter of the heart.

Many times, boys raised by super spiritual dads rebel and go off the deep end. They want to show the world how *unlike* their fathers they can be. I saw this occasionally at the university where I was a professor. Kids from the strictest, most conscientious Christian homes could sometimes delight in shocking my fellow faculty members by being as unchristian as they could be. Beneath the surface of this rebellion is usually a kid who just wants some space to be his own person and to form values of his own. We must try to help fathers understand this and ask them to loosen the reins just a bit.

Then there is . . .

The Real McCoy Dad

The "real McCoy" Dad is easy to spot. Characterized by supportiveness, acceptance, and love, he has confidence in his child-rearing abilities. Although he is quite aware that he will make mistakes, he tries to have a relaxed, balanced, and positive approach to fatherhood. This isn't to suggest that parenting comes easy to him. He may have come from a home where Dad was either gone most of the time or "checked-out" even when he was home.

This Dad's main secret is that he is determined to do what it takes to be an effective father. He takes it for granted that he must be open to God's direction and to learning from others, including his wife, so he can pass on wisdom, guidance, and nurturing to his son. He doesn't see his role ending when his boy hits eighteen, or twenty-one, or thirty—he's in this mentoring thing for life!

In short, the real McCoy Dad creates an environment where children thrive. Because the dad is involved in training, his authority is sometimes shared. Because he wants to be understood, he speaks and listens, so communication is stronger. He relies on listening, touching, understanding, and careful timing, so children are corrected in love. Because family members are free to tell each other how they feel, kids grow up with more confidence and greater emotional health. Isn't this what we aim for?

Mentor, Model, Teacher-for-Life

Much of what's involved in giving our sons what they need comes down to telling them what we think and feel. Thomas Lickona, author of *Raising Good Children*, calls this "teaching by telling."[3] Children can't read our minds. They want to know something about their moral, religious, and cultural heritage from us. They shout "talk to me!" with every tug of the pant leg, every jump in the lap, every tap on the shoulder. And with every "Hey, Dad . . . ?" Theirs is a confusing, mysterious, exciting, painful, and wonderful world. Your explanations, your values, your opinions are the only answers that matter—for now. Why squander your chance to impact them for life? Instead, use your time wisely.

Tory Hayden, an early childhood expert, reports that of 250 children interviewed, ages four to seventeen, almost all of them said they wished their families talked more.[4] Our sons do not only need to see us living lives that are worth imitating, they also need to hear *why* we do it—the values and beliefs that guide our actions and shape our words.

As mentors, as teachers-for-life, we become for our sons a reference point not only for how things are done, but why they are done.

Our power as fathers comes from practicing what we preach (and from discussing instead of preaching)! As Lickona reminds us, to "teach by telling," the father is explaining what he practices. I like that! As fathers, we have the biblical mandate of asking our sons to follow our example, especially as we learn to follow the example of the Lord Jesus Christ. And this can only happen if you are willing to make Christ your "Teacher-for-Life."

Andrew Murray, one of the most powerful spiritual men of the nineteenth century, gives the following illustration:

> I was very much struck some time ago by the practice a class in object lessons was put through. A picture was shown them, which they were told to look at very carefully. Then they had to shut their eyes and take time to think and remember everything they had seen. The picture was now removed, and the students had to tell everything they could remember. Again they were shown the picture, and they had to try to notice what they had not observed before. Again they had to shut their eyes, think and then tell what more they had noticed. And so once more, until every line of the picture had been taken in. As I looked at the keen interest with which the little eyes now gazed on the picture, and then were pressed so tightly shut as they tried to realize, take in, and keep what they had been looking at, I felt that if our Bible reading were more of such an object lesson, the unseen spiritual realities pictured to us in the Word would take much deeper hold of our inner life.[5]

Murray went on to say that we need to give "time for the substantial, spiritual reality that the Word of God contains to be lodged and rooted in the heart." What a wonderful observation—and very relevant to the work of the father as model to his son.

Putting It to Work

To lay the foundation for being a mentor, model, and teacher-for-life, consider the following ways of fostering a good, working relationship with your son:

1. Take time to set aside your preoccupations and feelings, and listen intently to your son without correcting or challenging his thinking.

2. Keep your body and facial expressions relaxed.

3. Establish eye contact.

4. Acknowledge your son's disappointments as well as triumphs by being physically there for him when he's on the mountaintop or crashing in the valley below.

5. Be flexible and adaptable in unplanned events—go with the flow!

6. Let your son know that he can discuss anything with you—from fears, anger, and hurts to joys, victories, and achievements.

7. Treat your son as a person—with all the dignity and respect you would want to receive.

8. Be comfortable with touching and showing affection, a pat on the head or your arm around his shoulder (hugs and kisses are okay, too!).

9. Remember that feelings should be accepted, not judged right or wrong. Help your son productively channel his frustrations or walk through his fears with you.

10. Avoid put-down messages, especially sarcasm or ridicule.

For Thought and Discussion

1. When you were growing up, how did you know your father loved you?

2. Of the five dads mentioned—the military dad, the hypocrite dad, the business partner dad, the super spiritual dad, and the real McCoy dad—which one comes the closest to your father, or was he a combination?

3. What kind of dad are you?

4. Consider Lee Iacocca's statement: "I've never heard of an executive who on his deathbed wished he'd spent more time at work."

3

What's Happening to My Son?

You can probably talk at length about things that interest you—how your computer's hard drive works, or your fuel-injection engine, or the muzzle-loader you built from a kit. Why not take a little time and effort to know about what's going on in your son's life? Huge changes are occurring as he moves through those passages from toddler to boy, to teenager, to young man.

From time to time your son will seem to go through revolutionary changes, almost overnight. The boy you thought you knew yesterday will not be the same boy next month. As dads, we can find ourselves thinking, *What's happening to my son?* Experts have made child development sound complicated and overly "psychological." Allow me to make it easy.

Basic Concepts and Principles of Child Development

It really helps to learn some basic concepts and principles of child development. I know, for example, that how I discipline my two-year-old must be different from how I discipline my seven-year-old. That's because what children are able to comprehend changes as they grow—and we need to grow and change with them.

Erik Erikson, a former professor of human development at Harvard University, provides us with an understanding of eight stages of development, from birth to old age.[1] He shows how our natural stages of development require us to adapt to eight milestones or turning points during the course of our child's lifespan.

If we understand what our sons are going through as they pass from infancy to adulthood, we can be more aware of how we, their fathers, can help them grow in strength, confidence, and spiritual health.

❖

Stage 1: Trust vs. Mistrust—This stage occurs from birth to approximately eighteen months. If our son has a feeling of physical comfort rather than fear or uncertainty during this time, he will develop a sense of *trust*. Ways to help a child move toward trust is to make his world as predictable and safe as possible, by having food available when he is hungry, attention when he is distressed, and by touching, holding, and looking at him on a consistent basis.

Stage 2: Autonomy vs. Shame and Doubt—This stage is most easily seen in children from eighteen months to three years of age. If a child feels in control of his own body, learning how to successfully "hold on" or "let go" with certain muscles, a sense of autonomy will develop. That's why potty-training should begin only when a child shows signs of readiness, usually not before two years. Shaming or belittling a child when he is not ready to grow in a certain area makes him clutch and become fear-filled.

Stage 3: Initiative vs. Guilt—This stage is highly visible in the three- to six-year-old child who loves to initiate activities, to enjoy a sense of achievement and competence. If children are allowed to step out into a new world of experience without constant pushing by us, a sense of initiative will develop.

Stage 4: Industry vs. Inferiority—This developmental phase shows itself from six years to the onset of puberty. Children begin to learn basic skills for independent living, which include reading, writing, and reasoning. Industry is the sense of accomplishment children feel when they are able to apply these skills to real-life situations, tasks, or problems. During this time, we should help our child develop academic and social skills. This is a good time to help him with homework, encourage him to play a musical instrument, and participate in Scouts or Little League, for example.

Stage 5: Identity vs. Role Confusion—This change shows up during adolescence and extends from the onset of puberty until the development of a mature identity. During this time, our sons begin to ask, "Who am I?" "What vocation or career will I choose?" "What values or beliefs will guide my life?" and "What kind of lifestyle will I have?"

It is during this time that our sons also experience significant bodily changes that may encourage him to start viewing himself as an adult, at least physically. Also, he has the mental capacity to begin dealing with notions of justice, truth, and equality. It is vital that we help our son think through values of self and of society. This is when it becomes especially important for us to help him think about a variety of life roles, such as student, brother, husband, father, and Christian.

Stage 6: Intimacy vs. Isolation—This stage involves a man's young adulthood. It is during this time that he contemplates his sense of commitment to others—including marriage and having children of his own. Usually this takes place only after your son has left home. The most important factor in his adaptation in this area will be his perception of your marriage and parenting skills.

Stage 7: Generativity vs. Stagnation—This stage leads from young adulthood to middle age. If your son, as an adult, shows care and concern for the next generation and a widening interest in work and ideas, he will not stagnate in life. Instead, he will develop generativity. He will make the healthy passage from the young-adult drive to "succeed" to middle-aged "fruitfulness."

Stage 8: Integrity vs. Despair—This stage centers around old age. It is the acceptance of one's life and the acceptance of the inevitability of death—coupled with feelings of dignity and meaning that insures against despair.

Cooperating With Your Son's Emotional Needs

Our sons have deep emotional needs. Erikson suggests that we fathers can benefit greatly by knowing how to build upon these seven developmental foundation stones: security, trust, love, acceptance, self-esteem, freedom, and limits.

Security—Basically, our boys need to feel safe and know that they are protected. They also need to believe that their homes, churches, and communities are stable and safe environments. Therefore, it will be essential that you, as his father, create a non-threatening world by being stable, reliable, and consistent. Be visible. Be supportive. Be available. And don't forget that physical and emotional affection are hugely important. Appropriate amounts of loving attention will go a long way in adding to your son's sense of security.

Trust—This emotional need will be very much dependent on your son's sense of security. If we add to security—being reliable with our time, keeping our promises, and being consistent in meeting our son's physical needs—then trust will more naturally occur.

Love—I am talking about unconditional, genuine love that helps your son see himself as a person of worth. A son who is loved by his father will see himself as lovable. (See 1 Corinthians 13.)

Acceptance—This emotional need, like love, must be unconditional. A son who is accepted believes he belongs in his family and is an important part of it. Affirm your son with the words, "I'm glad God gave you to me," or "Your mother and I feel so blessed that you are our son."

Self-esteem—Your son's self-esteem will be largely dependent upon the recognition, attention, and appreciation he receives from you. A son who holds himself in high regard is better able to accept the worth and potential of others.

Freedom—Your son will need your "okay" to explore, to be independent, and to make decisions on his own. Although he will need reasonable limits, your son will require the space to be himself. You may want to think through some issues now, like long hair, piercings, or—heaven forbid—tattoos. The key will be choosing your battles carefully.

Limits—The important distinction here is between slavery—making your son a slave of your will—and giving healthy guidance. Your son will not always be the best judge of his own interests, so some limitations and direction will be imperative. Establish boundaries early on and renegotiate the "rules" as your son matures.

Effective Communication

As fathers we can benefit by learning how to effectively communicate with children. Thomas Gordon says that parents should be involved in "active listening."[2] Active listening is when I try to hear not only the actual words my son says but also strive to understand his feelings. Thus, according to this approach, I listen to both the content and emotions of my son's communication. I also repeat back to my son what I think I heard him say. As a man, I am quick to rush through conversations and "get on with it," so I need to take time to help my son clarify his true feelings.

Dealing With Conflict

You will want to strive for a fair approach to resolving conflict. Every kid has a desire to be treated fairly. Even when my son was a preschooler, I learned to consider his point of view. Thomas Lickona describes the fairness approach to conflict as "expressing a viewpoint, listening to the other person, and finding common middle ground."[3] Some men want to resolve conflict by decree. I like the fact that Lickona's approach helps a child to reason morally—that is, to think about others' needs as well as his own. Otherwise, he'll grow up learning to be a "tyrant" rather than a wise "decision-maker."

Guidance as Discipline

And lastly, it will help us as teachers-for-life to understand the difference between punishment and discipline. Let's face it, there are times when you'd like to get really physical. But in reality, this kind of punishment is not always that effective. I have one child that responds to a little swat on the backside and another who, when spanked, hardly blinks.

We can't forget that we are disciplining our sons in order to teach what's right, not just to "blast" them for irritating us by doing wrong.

Guidance involves things that parents do to help a child control his behavior, take responsibility for the outcome of his actions and, as we have said earlier, help him consider the needs and feelings of others. Discipline is a form of parental guidance. Parents help their children recognize unacceptable behavior and replace it with more appropriate behavior.

Dr. Fredric P. Nelson, a Christian pediatrician in Philadelphia, tells me that discipline can be separated into various components, such as establishing boundaries, modeling and demonstration, imparting principles, practice, corrective actions, chastisement, and comforting. I have learned a lot from Fredric and feel grateful for all he has taught me. His thoughts and expertise form much of what I'll pass on to you now.

❖

Establishing Boundaries—A boundary limits your son's activity (such as a gate, a deterrent against biting, or denial of the keys to the family car). A boundary limits his attitudes (like requirements to say please or thank you, or not permitting bad language or back talk). Boundaries should fit the child—that is, they should be age-appropriate. You should also choose areas of confrontation in which you are sure to win. Write down and post good, positive boundaries in your son's room. Be sure he understands what behavior is good and healthy and what is not. And be sure to include consequences for wrongful activities or attitudes.

Modeling and Demonstration—Obviously, you are your son's first teacher who models and demonstrates all appropriate behaviors. Consider the following example. If you have a relative or friend coming over, show your son how to greet them. Even playact with your son the manners you expect him to use.

Imparting Principles—Principles give your son the rationale for specific teachings. A principle, then, can be applied to different situations and does not change. The principle of gravity, for example, applies to both spilled milk and falling off a bike. Break down the different areas of life and include the principles for right living. For instance, "We always speak respectfully and obey authorities." "We do not cheat or lie."

Telling your son that he shouldn't think bad jokes are funny, for example, is a sure way to lose. Helping him see that the humor value is not as great as the negative, degrading part of the joke is a better route. Or telling him he's forbidden to consider certain occupations you wouldn't choose for him can also be a loser. Instead, encourage him to explore his interests while helping him to take a mature look at what his job choice will mean in terms of education and future income possibilities.

Practice—Repetition trains the mind and body. And so, as fathers, we need to be the kind of coaches who are willing to observe, spend time to eliminate inappropriate behavior, and help our sons practice the appropriate activity or attitude. For instance, if you or your wife ask your son to do chores, and he snaps back, "I'm busy!" you can say, "The correct response is, 'I'll do it right now.'"

Corrective Actions—When you observe a wrong, determine the specific error, demonstrate the correct activity or attitude, initiate the practice drill.

Chastisement—Only as a last resort, such as in cases of willful disobedience, rebellion, or disrespect (and I might add, when danger to the child is probable—such as running into the street or touching/playing with electrical outlets), I recommend a moderate amount of corporal discipline. Be careful, not abusive, either physically or verbally. "Time out"—a technique that isolates the child on a chair or in one room in the house for a specific period of time—can also be used effectively.

Comforting Follows Chastisement—It is wise to follow discipline with taking your son into your arms and reassuring him with the words, "I love you. Let's remember what we learned here and move on."

❖

As a former professor of human development and family studies for Abilene Christian University, I had always reminded my students that nearly 85 percent of a child's personality is formed by the time he or she is six years old. But the development is far from over. That's why learning the best ways to better communicate, discipline, and meet our sons' emotional needs is so important.

Larger Influences—Just before we leave this chapter on our sons' development, we need to consider the wider range of influences that he will be exposed to—particularly from adults (for example, the relationship between our son and other male family members). Also, his teachers, coaches, scout leaders, tutors, or trainers. Other men will make impressions on our sons. We need to monitor every influence in their lives and ask, "How helpful is this relationship or experience to my son's overall well-being?" We need to stay involved and find out what kinds of attitudes and habits are being modeled by other men.

A friend of mine reports that his son one day came out with a shocking racial slur—quickly followed by a degrading comment about women. "Where did you hear that?" my friend demanded. "Well, Uncle Jack says that stuff all the time," his son retorted. Quick correction—for the boy and Uncle Jack—cuts off the bad influence of an unhealthy attitude.

The church you choose to attend while your son is growing up is another major influence you will want to consider carefully. Be honest and think about whether your congregation is grace-oriented or legalistic. Does it emphasize affection and forgiveness, or promote a works-oriented spirituality where a person strives to merit or earn God's love and approval? The more negative the church, the more potentially damaging it will be to your son's level of self-esteem. I'd recommend praying about this and talking it over with your wife and family. Find out how the congregation you attend affects them and their view of God. Use the time to talk about what you really believe as a family. Who knows, you might find yourselves well on the way to having your first family devotional!

In conclusion, you *can* use your father power wisely and effectively to shape your son's spirit—for life!

For Thought and Discussion

1. When you were young, what caused you to feel important and valuable?

2. Do you listen intently to what your son is trying to tell you?

3. What kind of discipline did your father use most of the time? Was it effective? What could you change about your own method of discipline?

4. What aspects of this discussion of growth and development helped you understand your son better? How can you use this knowledge to help him become stronger, healthier?

4

The Bird That Gets the Worm

Preparing Your Son to Work

As fathers, we sometimes think it's our job to prepare our sons for a specific vocation. Say, to become a doctor, mechanic, builder, or accountant. But, in fact, college or vocational education can do that much better than you or I can. My goal in this chapter is to focus on how your son can develop integrity, self-discipline, and the proper motivation to be successful in any job he attempts to do.

Jesus's life was lived with purpose. He was very intentional about the things He did, the people He saw, the miracles He performed, and even the words He spoke. He lived His life by design and not by accident. He knew what He was about, and that fact alone led Him to the cross despite numerous obstacles—not the least of which was Satan. No doubt Satan wanted to steer Jesus off-course from His intended destiny, and the temptation of Christ seems to have been designed by Satan with this in mind (Matthew 4:1–11).

The temptation is the same for each of us—to live life by happenstance as opposed to living it deliberately, with goals in view.

It's absolutely essential that we, as fathers and mentors, relentlessly live our lives with purpose. To do this, you and I must be convinced that we were created for a reason. Although that reason may include our vocation, work should never be an end in itself. As someone has wisely discerned, "There is no future in any job. The future is in the person who holds the job."

Again, this was true of Jesus, who was chosen by God to save the world. Only Jesus could have been qualified to accomplish the redemptive work of God. God's plan called for a person who was sinless and who would voluntarily bear our sins in His body on our behalf (see 1 Peter 2:22–24). This, of course, meant that Jesus was the right person for the job that had to be done.

Likewise, we can help our sons to understand that it's not so much finding the right kind of job as being the right kind of person that matters. Many employers understand that the character of a man is as important as the job he is trained to do, because it inevitably affects the job. Honest, hardworking men and women are wanted everywhere.

A story is told of the late Sam Walton, founder of Walmart. Walton had just hired a senior executive for his company, and to celebrate, he took the young man to lunch. As was Sam's custom, instead of choosing a fancy restaurant, he picked a local cafeteria. While they were in line waiting to pay for the food, Mr. Walton noticed his hireling stuffing pats of butter into his suit-coat pocket. The butter pats cost mere pennies, and Mr. Walton was footing the bill—which made this petty thievery seem all the more senseless to Sam. During lunch Mr. Walton withdrew his offer to the young man, citing the stolen butter as his reason. The now unemployed senior executive was dumbfounded, and unfortunately could never quite understand why such a small—to him, even insignificant—thing, like taking a few pats of butter, could cost him his job. To Walton, it was an obvious character flaw—a small crack that could well lead to an even bigger ethical rupture later on.

Our goal as mentors is primarily to train our sons to be worthy of a position. Character is what makes the difference. To be worthy is to deserve a job or position. When we study the word "deserving," there is associated with it the concept of merit. When I am responsible with menial tasks, the door may be open for me to be responsible for even greater assignments. Unfortunately, many employers today observe that too many young men believe the world *owes* them the best jobs, the most esteemed positions, and the most prominent titles, whether or not they have demonstrated that they deserve them.

This was true even of the disciples. You may remember how they argued about who among them would be the greatest of all. (See Mark 9:33–37.) Jesus taught them that spiritual greatness means being a servant—that is, choosing to take on responsibility for the leadership, care, and well-being of others.

Beyond Ourselves

You see, Jesus taught this great principle: that you and I and our sons have a place and a purpose far greater than us. Sure, fishing is a fine profession (although tax collecting may not be!), but Jesus connected His men to a greater sense of purpose. How many men do you know who feel purposeless and empty? We must first teach our sons that God has a purpose for them. A sense of purpose will help motivate them to do a worthy job. Jesus states that one of the reasons God sent Him into the world was to serve (Matthew 20:28). And that because of His service—dying on the cross—"God exalted him" (Acts 5:31). Even the apostle Paul draws a correlation between servanthood and advancement when he writes, "Those who have served well gain an excellent standing" (1 Timothy 3:13).

To teach our sons how to serve will be the basis, or the foundation, of a greater purpose—achieving success in whatever profession they choose. It also will establish them as valuable witnesses to help the world, and those with whom they work, understand the true nature of Christianity. God did not abandon us to meaningless toil—this was the result of the curse (Genesis 3:17–19). The heavenly Father's mission for you and me is the only thing that gives reason and meaning to our being. That mission includes making known the God of the universe, and we do that by diligence, commitment, service, our disposition, and our conduct.

Jesus, again, is our example here. Remember the Last Supper when He wrapped a towel around His waist and washed the feet of His disciples? (See John 13:1–17.) Peter objected to this because of Christ's divine origin. He falsely concluded that God doesn't wash feet. Jesus, who was God, obviously was trying to get Peter to understand something about majesty that eluded him: The greatest among them would be the servant of all! When he was younger, my greatest wish for my son was that he would become a member of the "Order of the Towel," knowing that by serving God while serving others, he would have one of the greatest keys to success. Or, to say it another way, when he is free in his attitude to serve God in all circumstances, he will be free from the bullying or demands of any boss—free to do the best job he can, knowing he has only one final judge. That's true freedom! This is the kind of servant's heart you and I are called to model for our sons. And we can do this in the simplest of ways.

When I am seen washing dishes with my wife or preparing the evening meal, I am telling my son who Christ is and what attitude he must take on. When my son sees me cleaning the church building, raking the yard, and shoveling snow on the walkways, I am telling him what Christ was like and what attitude he must adopt. When he sees me visiting the sick, taking the Word of God to the local prison, or feeding the poor in our community, I am showing him God as He really is!

There was a man in our parish who was well-educated, well-traveled, and highly respected in his field, and yet he was the one who repaired the toilets in our church building, stripped and waxed the floors, and did general maintenance on a regular basis. We were the only church I knew of who had an MBA senior-executive mowing the parish lawn! Is it any wonder, then, when it came time to appoint a president for our congregation's Board of Trustees that this man was chosen? He deserved to be our chief executive officer because he was and is a servant who continues to be responsible for all those unwanted, undesirable tasks.

You and I both know men in the working world who can think of nothing more than their own agenda and personal needs. They may even be successful, for now. But self-seekers have a way of getting ruined in the end. Men who are there for others are sought and valued.

We can train our sons today to be the valued and sought-after employees of tomorrow—young men who do not *demand* position, authority, and big bucks, but rather those who *command* these benefits because of their character.

Integrity

Integrity is the quality of being complete, or undivided—when someone has integrity, he proves worthy of our trust. A bridge that has structural integrity can be trusted to hold up under our feet or carry our car safely to the other side. Teaching our sons to have integrity—that is, to be whole, single in purpose, and undivided—will prepare them well for any future employment.

Men who have integrity are dependable! These guys can be trusted to show up for work on time, meet deadlines, be there in a crisis, and even go the extra mile if that's what it takes to get the job done. Unfortunately, people aren't always born dependable. Most often, dependability is learned.

To help your son learn dependability, put him on a weekly work schedule. Make sure to assign things he can do after school, such as cleaning his room, putting out the trash, helping to set the dinner table, and caring for younger siblings. Make up a chart that lists his weekly chores and let him be responsible to complete them. You may need to sit down with him and figure out a timetable for each activity. Being punctual is another indispensable part of being dependable. When all of his responsibilities are completed, either that day or by the end of the week, reward him. Let him choose an activity—such as playing catch in the backyard, playing a board game, taking him to the movies, or just hanging out together. It's not so important what you do, but that you do it together! Or you may wish to offer him a small sum of money, appropriate to the amount of work and time spent.

Another thing you can do to help your son learn dependability is to allow him to experiment with long-term projects around the house. Obviously, these would not fit into his after-school work schedule, but would be reserved for Saturdays and days off from school. It is so important that he find out what he's good at doing so that he'll be enthusiastic and throw himself into his work. A powerful esteem-builder is your son's ability to master new skills, receive recognition for a job well done, and gain confidence to do a particular task entirely on his own.

For example, I found that my son, Patrick, loved to strip wood, sand it, and then paint it. It wasn't hard, therefore, to get him to be dependable with a job when it was something he enjoyed doing. Encouraging my son's sense of industry made him feel capable and useful. And when a boy brings his whole being into a weekend project he loves, he does an even better job than usual.

Encourage your son to experiment with various projects, such as fixing up a classic car or repairing a motorcycle. Or help him learn to use tools as you work together to make general repairs around the house. In these ways, your son might even find a career path that suits him. We never know what will spark our son's interest until we let him try a number of things. And doing what he likes to do can be more motivational than a paycheck. Just ask the guy who hates his job. He'll tell you how he does damaging things to deaden the pain, like drinking or gambling, or how he blows money on "toys" to fill in the emptiness or salve the anger.

When your son is trying out his newfound abilities, don't compare his work to that of other siblings. Having an older brother and sister, I can relate to the misguided effort of my parents who, when comparing me to my brother or sister, tried to communicate that I could do something. Unfortunately, all I heard was, "You're not as good as Billy or Dee." Rather, compare your son to his past performance: "You've done better" or "I see improvement."

You can also teach your son that God will help him as he develops skills, for as Paul said, "I can do everything through him who gives me strength" (Philippians 4:13). This can be a wonderful confidence builder as he learns to rely on God for skill, integrity, and dependability. Have him journey through the Word with you to reflect on God's promises to guide him along life's path and give him wisdom and ability.

Self-Discipline

According to a *USA Today* article, 90 percent of Americans make New Year's resolutions. Experts tell us, however, that only one in five people follow through on their vows to lose weight, get out of debt, or develop a daily devotional life. Helping your son to be self-disciplined enough to do what needs to be done is no small task. To be self-disciplined is to know one's whims, patterns, preferences, strengths, and weaknesses. To know them so well, in fact, that, according to Paul and Sarah Edwards, who are gurus of the work-at-home movement, "We can literally feed ourselves the exact words, schedule, food, routines, and resources we need to nourish our competence and enable us to operate consistently at our best."[1]

Our mentoring as dads can begin with simple things that connect with our sons' interests. This can include helping your son develop a tailor-made training schedule that includes a practice routine or workout with regard to his favorite sport or chosen athletic endeavor; helping him find information about cars, animals, computers, music, oceanography, or whatever else interests him; helping him develop a diet that focuses on good nutrition and balanced meals so he can stay in shape; or helping him have a daily devotional life that includes beginning the day with prayer and Bible study. These habits, if developed early, will form a solid foundation for your son to build on physically, mentally, and spiritually throughout his life. They will help him gain the sense of well-being and focus that he will need to stay on track through adulthood.

What we're talking about is training in self-motivation.

Again, I look to Jesus as the ultimate example. There is no doubt that He had the self-motivation to follow through on what His heavenly Father wanted Him to do—a motivation so powerful that He could go all the way to the cross.

This self-motivation came from His relationship with His Father. From birth, Jesus was determined to do God's will, obviously with the capable help of His earthly father, Joseph.

Jesus was really God-motivated. Because He wanted to do whatever God told Him to do, He fasted for forty days, said no to Satan's temptations, rose early for prayer, healed the multitudes even when He was tired, and eventually suffered the unjust agonies of the cross.

The Proper Motivation

A. C. Green, a two-time NBA champion, in his autobiography *Victory,* writes, "Purify your motives and your heart. Get a pure desire for victory that wants victory for the Lord's sake, not just for your own." He continues:

> Pastor Dave Elian taught me a lot about the Word and building character. First I learned about serving others. We were a small group, so everyone had to pitch in. Even though I was the star athlete, I cleaned toilets, both in my church and in my apartment. Once again I felt ownership. As my "star" rose, work like that helped keep my feet on the ground and my head out of the clouds. I realized I was always going to be a person as well as an athlete. I also learned that unless you're willing to serve, you cannot earn the right to lead.
>
> Pastor Dave taught us about the importance of daily Bible reading and prayer. . . . God honored our obedience. . . . Pastor Dave also emphasized keeping our word. He lived with integrity and challenged us to a high level of integrity ourselves.
>
> "The honesty of a man's heart, the depth of his manly character, is shown by how he keeps his word," he said. . . . He taught us to honor whatever we said we would do, to control our tongues and to not make careless promises. . . .

If we didn't make it to a 6:00 A.M. prayer meeting after saying we'd go, we were rudely awakened by a telephone call. . . . Pastor Dave drilled integrity into our lives not out of legalism but out of respect for ourselves, others, and God.[2]

I think Andrew Murray said it best when he wrote, "Acknowledge the sacred right of ownership Christ has in you, His blood-bought ones. And let nothing prevent you from answering: *Yes, dear Lord, as far as is allowed to a child of dust, I will be like You. I am entirely Yours. I must, I will, in all things bear Your image. . . .*"

The proper motivation, then, comes from a heart fully yielded to God in all things—this includes one's vocational aspirations. We should strive to be a Christian carpenter, a Christian lawyer, a Christian teacher, a Christian politician, a Christian plumber, a Christian bank executive, a Christian doctor or nurse, whatever the case may be. Yes, even a Christian NBA all-star athlete.

The proper motivation will also come when we help our sons understand that work is God's provision for His people, and as such should be done as unto the Lord. "Whatever you do, work at it with all your heart, as working for the Lord, not for men" (Colossians 3:23). This will help our sons deal with that I-couldn't-care-less attitude. When he is taught to regard all employment "as working for the Lord," he will have the proper motivation to take his work seriously. Jesus worked as a carpenter. The apostle Paul worked as a tentmaker. A Christian man, whether he is a janitor or a doctor, works for God.

Basics That Never Fail

Helping our sons take responsibility early in life will prepare them well for the workplace in the future. Two kinds of responsibility should be emphasized: responsibility for themselves, and responsibility toward others.

Taking responsibility for themselves may include personal grooming, exercise, care of the family car with each use (including filling the gas tank), taking care of personal possessions, doing homework assignments on time, earning money and saving some by taking a part-time job outside the home, and tithing. In our household, Patrick had four cups for his money. One was labeled "for God," which contained his tithe (ten percent of everything he earned plus monetary gifts). One was labeled "long-term savings," which could not be tapped into. One was labeled "short-term savings," which helped pay for specialty items or gifts for Christmas or birthdays. The fourth was labeled "immediate use," which covered day-to-day expenses such as snacks, etc.

Responsibility for others may include caring for a pet for someone; watching or playing with a sibling or helping to dress a younger sibling; or doing household chores, such as cleaning or helping in the kitchen. When I was growing up, we were required to shovel snow and mow the lawn for the widow next door. My wife's father, a pastor, used to take Rachel with him to nursing homes and the hospital to visit the elderly, and to in-home Bible studies that he led. I believe such experiences paved the way for my wife's benevolence and goodwill that characterizes her work as a private school-teacher today.

Stephen Covey, in his bestselling book *The Seven Habits of Highly Effective People,* suggests that if we really want to see our sons do a job responsibly, we must give them a clear, mutual understanding of what needs to be accomplished, concentrating on *what* not *how, results* not *method.* He says to be patient and spend time helping your son visualize the desired result: Let him see it, describe it, talk about what the results will look like, and when they must be completed. He calls it the "Green and Clean" method of delegation. I'll let him explain.

Some years ago, I had an interesting experience in delegation with my son. My seven-year-old, Stephen, volunteered to take care of the yard. Before I actually gave him the job, I began a thorough training process. I wanted him to have a clear picture in mind of what a well-cared-for yard was like, so I took him next door to our neighbor's.

"Look son," I said. "See how our neighbor's yard is green and clean? That's what we're after: green and clean. Now come look at our yard. See all the colors? That's not it; that's not green. Green and clean is what we want. Now, how you get it clean is up to you. You're free to do it any way you want to, except paint it. But I'll tell you how I'd do it if it were up to me."

"How would you do it, Dad?"

"I'd turn on the sprinklers. But you may want to use buckets or a hose. It makes no difference to me. All we care about is that the color is green. Okay?"

"Okay."

"Now let's talk about 'clean,' son. Clean means no messes around—no paper, strings, bones, sticks, or anything that messes up the place. . . . Let's just clean up half the yard right now and look at the difference."

So we got two paper sacks and picked up one side of the yard. "Now look at the other side. See the difference? That's called clean.

"Now, before you decide whether or not you're going to take the job, let me tell you a few more things. Because when you take the job, I don't do it anymore. It's your job. It's called a stewardship. Stewardship means 'a job with trust.' I trust you to do the job, to get it done. . . . You're the boss. . . ."[3]

Trust is one of the highest forms of motivation, says Covey. Whenever I trust my son to do a job entirely on his own, it brings out the best in him. As Covey reminds us, it will take time and patience. You may have to help your son several times before he's completely on his own, but soon his level of competence will rise to the occasion. The idea is to not do the task for your son, but—with the proper training and development—to empower him to do it.

Another concept to help your son grasp is what we call "balancing frugality with extravagance." I'm thinking about frugality as a way of life, but tempered by moments of carefully planned extravagance for special family celebrations, such as Christmas, birthdays, anniversaries, Thanksgiving, baptisms, weddings, and the like. The idea is to help our sons know the importance of living well within their means—i.e., teaching them how to develop a budget and securing for them a savings account, etc.—but also showing them how to spend money in a very calculated way that tells our families that they are deserving of our hard-earned dollars.

Lastly, take a walk through the Bible with your son. Highlight the following books or passages of Scripture with him on a regular basis:

1. Read the book of Proverbs, which speaks out against sloth or slack and in favor of being diligent and hard-working.

2. Read Paul's warning in 2 Thessalonians 3:10: "If a man will not work, he shall not eat."

3. Read about the parable of the talents in Matthew 25:14–30, which talks about God's expectations regarding the abilities he has given us.

4. Review Paul's counsel that equates work with serving the Lord, not men (Colossians 3:23–24).

5. Review sins that pertain to the marketplace—pilfering (Titus 2:9–10); slackness (2 Thessalonians 3:11–12); being a man-pleaser (Colossians 3:22).

6. Study "the wife of noble character" in Proverbs 31:10–31, who "works with eager hands" and "gets up while it is still dark" and is "clothed with strength and dignity."

7. Read Genesis 2:2, where God rested after His work. Keep the Sabbath a day set apart for rest, devotion to God, and family.

For Thought and Discussion

1. In Stephen Covey's book *The Seven Habits of Highly Effective People,* he provides a paradigm of delegation, called "Green and Clean." The idea is to train our sons to be stewards who are trusted, their own boss governed by a conscience committed to agreed-upon results. How will such an approach help prepare your sons for the workplace?

2. How does the Indian proverb "Give a man a fish and he'll eat for a day; teach a man to fish and he'll eat for a lifetime" apply to the task of preparing our sons for the workplace?

3. Covey says, "No amount of technical administrative skill in laboring . . . can ever make up for a lack of nobility of personal character. . . . It is at a very essential, one-on-one level that we live the primary laws of love and life."[4] Do you agree? Explain.

5

"All Work and No Play . . ."

Helping Your Son to Enjoy Life

I can remember not even wanting to go. Rachel, my wife, thought it would be a good idea to take the kids to one of the "Great Adventure" theme parks. We were living in Texas, and I wanted to stay home and let the kids escape the heat wave in the backyard kiddie pool. I had rigged up a sliding board so that Patrick and Kayla could slip and slide into the cool water. The kids were happy. I was happy. I had my lounge chair and my radio. What else could we possibly want?

But Rachel insisted we load up the car and head for Dallas for two days of amusement park rides and sideshows. Of course, the kids were all in favor of it. They had everything they needed right in their own backyard, but they agreed to ride for two hours in a cramped car to an overcrowded carnival, stand in long lines to ride the Texas Giant roller-coaster, and risk getting sick on overpriced food and drinks.

Go figure! It was a conspiracy: three votes in favor of two days of overheated amusement park madness, and one vote in favor of a quiet, cool, relaxed vacation at home.

The park was everything I feared it would be: expensive tickets that put a huge dent in my wallet, unreasonably priced souvenirs, and parking that cost an arm and a leg. (Shouldn't parking be included in the price of the ticket?) Well, I was letting everything get to me, and I must admit I was becoming increasingly more difficult to be around.

Rachel pulled me over to the side so the kids couldn't hear. "Quit being such a bear, Michael," she whispered. "We're missing out on all the fun. Maybe we could be doing something else—cheaper. But open your eyes. You are spoiling it for your children."

She was right. So I decided to get "in gear" and show my family how to have a good time. I really got crazy. I rode the bumper cars. I ate cotton candy. Then we rode the Texas Giant.

Changing my attitude saved the weekend. By letting go and loosening up, I gave my family permission to relax and have a good time, too. Instead of three against one, we were now unified and freed-up to enjoy life together.

It's true that, as fathers, we have the power to set the tone. If we're enjoying life, chances are our families are, too. So much of what will be our sons' experience growing up is dependent upon our own attitude. I've met a lot of dads who take life too seriously, perhaps even take themselves too seriously. They find it hard to relax. They're always worried about looking professional or being "adult." Their kids become uptight, too. And an uptight kid grows up to be a very rigid adult.

Back when Patrick was a preschooler, I'd come home from work and it was time to play. He'd grab my hand and we'd run into his bedroom and get under the bed—we were hiding from dinosaurs! It was awkward at times when one of my students from the university would show up and my suit would be a rumpled mess from being under Patrick's bed—but hey, that's just part of being a daddy!

I remember the time I asked my father to watch Patrick for a few minutes while Rachel and I went next door. When we got back, neither of them was in sight. As we searched the house, I heard faint laughter coming from my son's room. I swung open the closet door and found my dad, holding Patrick's hand in the dark.

"Dad, what are you doing?" I asked.

"Pterodactyls, Michael! Pterodactyls!" he replied.

How many men do you know who need to lighten up? It is important to know how to have fun. Developing your son's creativity and spontaneity will help him enjoy life, as well as prepare him to be a fun person to be around. You have a big hand in teaching your son how to meet life's challenges with good humor and a carefree attitude.

Imagination

One important way of helping your son to enjoy life is developing his imagination. Start when he's young and introduce him to the meaning and importance of fairy tales. "Children meet the problems of the world with their imaginations," says author Walter Wangerin Jr., "and the fairy tale honors, feeds and abets the imagination."[1]

Stories that stir the imagination can also be moral stories that anchor our sons to what is right and good. With this in mind, I'd like to suggest that you choose stories to read to your young sons that will help them open up to the world of imagination. For instance, fairy tales like *Snow White, Cinderella,* and *Pinocchio* depict goodness overcoming evil in a world of enchantment. Hans Christian Andersen's *The Steadfast Tin Soldier* is a great story for boys about courage and love. *The Chronicles of Narnia,* by C. S. Lewis, teach marvelous lessons of faith. The series can be your son's passport to fantastic lands and extraordinary events.

For older boys who like to read, I recommend westerns, such as Jim Walker's WELLS FARGO TRAIL series, and the SAGA OF THE SIERRAS series by Brock and Bodie Thoene. And you can't beat great books like *Johnny Tremain,*[2] *The Red Badge of Courage,*[3] or *The Call of the Wild*[4] if you want to whet a boy's appetite for adventure and bravery.

Another way to stir young imaginations is storytelling. Ruth Stafford Peale, wife of the late Norman Vincent Peale, wrote about her husband's storytelling:

When our children were small, for example, Norman spent hours telling them stories that he made up on the spur of the moment, right out of his head. This generally took place at the dinner table and the children could hardly wait. I remember one whole series that went on for months about three imaginary characters named Larry, Harry, and Parry. These remarkable young people had a magic airplane that they kept in their pocket until they needed it. If they wanted to go anyplace they would take the airplane, blow on it and, like magic, it became large enough for them to climb aboard and take off. They would soar away to investigate a big, billowy cloud, or to fight with giants, or to live in the forest in the treetops, or to rescue princesses in distant lands. The magic airplane was very real and exciting . . . to our children.[5]

Another way to stir imagination is to plan a trip, a hike, or a small building project together.

"They were getting too old for story time," said Bill, the father of two teenage boys.

I had to find something that would stir their imaginations—and at the same time be physically challenging enough to hold their interest and keep them engaged. So I decided we should all take up wilderness exploring. It wasn't easy. The boys were already in shape. But me, that was another story. I had to lose an initial twenty-five pounds. I stuck with it, though.

We got a friend from church to help us train. He was an expert in this kind of thing. He knew the right clothing and equipment to buy. Plus, he was really safety-conscious— that made my wife feel a whole lot better. Especially when she heard he'd agreed to serve as a tour guide for our first trip.

We took the Rawah Wilderness, a part of the Roosevelt National Forest in Colorado. While we were hiking up the West Branch Junction, we spotted a bald eagle circling high above Blue Lake. It was the first time, outside of a zoo, my boys and I had ever seen an eagle. That evening, after we had set up camp and built a fire, the boys pulled out pencils and drawing pads and tried to capture on paper the sight of that magnificent bird.

Creativity

Helping your son develop creativity is another way of preparing him to enjoy life. A study showed that people who took different routes to work each day stayed more creative than those who took the same way. Creativity begins with breaking your routine and not being afraid to try out new things. Here are some suggestions on how to jump-start your son's creative juices.

> Listen to all forms of music. The folk songs of America can provide your son with a sense of cultural and historical identity. Expand your horizons by trying out music from other cultures and ethnic origins.

> Go to plays and live performances of all kinds. Many local theaters or music fairs offer a variety of children's entertainment apart from their regularly scheduled adult programs. Check your local newspaper for times and locations.

> Have a stock of art supplies at home. Be sure to include construction paper, glue, markers, paint, safety scissors, and other odds and ends. Relax, and don't get nervous about the mess that's created while a project is being completed. And remember to wear old shirts in case things get a little out of hand.

> Show him how to make a fort or clubhouse out of anything on-hand. On rainy days it can be kitchen chairs with blankets draped over them. Outside, it can be discarded planks of wood, plywood, or cardboard boxes.

Visit museums of all kinds; try a planetarium and the science institute. Find out if there are any archaeological digs or building restorations going on near you.

Encourage your son to play a musical instrument, especially one you know how to play. Have plenty of sing-along songs on hand.

Help your son write a book or story of his own; use a computer, and help him with the cover art and binding.

If your son is the outdoors type, help him plan his own backyard or woodlot adventure. Help him figure out everything he'll need for "survival." Invite another boy or boys to share the adventure.

Tim Hansel, president of Summit Expedition, in his book *Creative Fathering,* recommends developing a backyard or living-room Olympics.

All it takes is a little bit of creativity, a roll of masking tape, a wristwatch that measures seconds, a yardstick or tape measure and a few extra things like paper plates, sheets of paper and felt-tip markers. If you want, prepare make-believe gold, silver and bronze medals to hang around the necks of the winners. It all depends on how fancy you want to be. Your home-style Olympics can include such events as a standing one-foot broad jump, a standing two-foot broad jump, or a discus throw with a paper plate. If you're in the backyard, use a large rock for a shot put. If you're in your living room, use a wad of paper. Set up obstacle courses and see who can cover them in the best time.[6]

Spontaneity

To help your son be spontaneous, you need to be spontaneous yourself—like the father who used to keep a "why not?" notebook at the office to write down unconventional and even bizarre ideas that occurred to him during the day, such as why not camp out in the living room with tents made from blankets? Or why not play flashlight tag in the house with all the lights off?

The key here is simply to do something out of the ordinary. Catch your son off-guard! Take him by complete surprise! Wake him up in the middle of the night to go climb trees or look for shooting stars; show up at school with tickets to a movie matinee.

Let me tell you about the church elder who plays "dart wars" with his twelve kids. Bill Parker is a highly successful businessman, but when he wants to have fun, everyone better watch out! You can be over at this guy's house and not know when he'll just drop everything and call out, "Let's play dart wars!" All of a sudden, kids and adults are scrambling for their rubber-tipped darts and dart guns. From what I hear, you'd better be a pretty good shot if you want to survive an evening with the Parker family.

Spontaneity can actually prepare your son to be a great husband, because the element of surprise goes a long way in keeping romance alive in a marriage. Listen to one father's incredible inventiveness and creativity that led to spontaneous fun for the whole family.

"When the boys were between the ages of five and fifteen, we did a lot of camping, boating, fishing and water-skiing," says Mac, a sixty-seven-year-old grandfather from Southern

California. One evening when his oldest son, Todd, was eighteen, Mac had a suggestion for the whole family: "Why don't we go around the world?"

The year was 1972, and Mac's construction business was going great guns. Why not take an extended trip? Todd was about to graduate, his brother Tommy could continue his high school education by correspondence, and the two younger boys, Keith and Denny, well, they would just have to miss a year of school.

"We really saw how other cultures lived," says Mac, "and it sure made the kids appreciative of what they had. It's too bad all families can't afford it, because it was the most rewarding thing we did as a family. Now my sons all want to do it with their children."

"Because of that around-the-world trip, my brother Denny decided to go into full-time medical missions service. It was a real eye-opening experience," says Todd.[7]

The benefit to you when you become an imaginative, creative, and spontaneous dad is that you release the pressures of the day in a more constructive way than kicking the dog or yelling at your kids. You don't have to be the family "heavy" anymore. Rather than have your son sweat out the words, "Wait till your father gets home!" he can relax knowing that when dad opens the front door, it signals a time of fun for the whole family.

The benefit to your son when you become a fun dad is that correction is easier to take when he's hearing it from a guy with whom he leg-wrestles, because he knows you really like him in spite of the fact that he just soaked his sister with a hose and made her scream! You'll also break the inertia that is the killjoy of fun. Your son will find family life so much more enjoyable when you become that I-can't-say-what-will-happen-next kind of dad.

For Thought and Discussion

1. When you were growing up, did your father ever display a sense of humor? Was he imaginative, creative, spontaneous—and in what ways?
2. Would your son describe you as imaginative or dull; creative or non-inventive; spontaneous or rehearsed; relaxed or tense; fun or serious?
3. What can you do to have more fun with your son at home?

6

Seek Ye First
the Kingdom of God

Helping Your Son to Be a Disciple of Christ

One of the high points of life is the moment we come to know Jesus Christ as our Savior and Lord. I'm sure you can look back and remember the time Christianity really took hold of your heart.

I was fifteen. It was 1971, just after a Billy Graham Crusade, and sitting there in that huge coliseum, surrounded by thousands of people, made me feel so insignificant. But Graham's message made me feel important in the eyes of God. "Christ loves you," he told the crowd. But I heard, "Christ loves Michael." Before I knew it, I was getting out of my seat and walking forward at Graham's invitation, together with a herd of new converts. My mother was there, and my older brother, too. It was a night I will never forget.

But what came next? How did this fledgling, personal revival translate into a lifestyle that produced healthy, spiritual fruit? This is what my mentor and surrogate "spiritual father," Dr. Tom Schlaf, was faced with—the full challenge of committed discipleship that moved me from the "believing" side to the "behaving" side of faith.

How a man prepares his son to be a devout disciple of Christ is what we will focus on in this chapter. This discipleship includes having a quiet time; meditating on the Word with a view to applying it to life; developing a personal prayer life; understanding and experiencing worship as praise, thanksgiving, and confession; and finding the friendship of other Christians as a way of life.

First Things First

There is an incredible concept found in the writings of the apostle Paul and elsewhere in the New Testament that we need to grasp. Paul calls it the "sanctification of the believer" (see Romans 15:16; 1 Corinthians 1:2; 1 Thessalonians 4:3; 5:23; 2 Thessalonians 2:13). Sanctification occurs over a long period of time, whereas salvation is a one-time event. The idea here is that every day after my conversion, I am to let God show me parts of my life that need to be changed from my character to His character. When I see my weaknesses, failures, and sins, I go to Him for empowering grace and forgiveness by confessing and repenting of wrongdoing. I let God put the fruit of Christian character in its place (see Galatians 5:22–23). *Sanctification* simply means that little by little I become "set apart" from my old way of responding to life by the slow, powerful, determined work of the Holy Spirit in my daily experiences.

As a man before God, you can cooperate with the Holy Spirit as "Supreme Mentor" to your son. You need to trust that God will give your believing son insight on a regular basis, both through the Bible and through his conscience (see John 14:25–26; 16:12–13). He will cause your son to ask, "Is it wrong to do this?" "What is the right thing to do?" or, "What should my Christian attitude be?" In these instances, the Holy Spirit will bring insight—maybe a Scripture or a memory of what you, his dad, would say or do—to help lead him down the right path.

Though you and I can be spiritual coaches, it is the Holy Spirit, then, and no one else, who will give your son the power to live a life that's different and godly. If we teach our sons to yield to this process and not ignore the inner promptings of the Holy Spirit, then God will mold them into strong men of good character.

The familiar illustration is that of a worker in a foundry who is turning molten metal into something useful. As he stands watch over it, occasionally he removes some of the dross—or impure material—as it bubbles to the surface. He knows the job is done when he can see his own face perfectly reflected, like a mirror, on the surface of the molten metal. So it is with the work of the Holy Spirit. God continues to cleanse and change us until He sees the image of Jesus Christ reflected in us, His sons.

The key is to help our sons yield to the work of the Holy Spirit, versus exerting their own will over sin. Paul the apostle knew well the tactics of mere legalists who were trying to force Christians to abstain from wrongdoing: "Do not handle! Do not taste! Do not touch!" (Colossians 2:21). He knew, however, that "such regulations indeed have an appearance of wisdom," but lack any power "in restraining sensual indulgence" (v. 23).

Paul likened the Christian life to a race. He talked about disciplining himself much the same way an athlete trained for the Olympic games in Rome. Teaching your sons some simple spiritual disciplines is important. Disciplines like a quiet time, study of the Word, prayer, and fellowship will help our sons yield their lives over to the heavenly Father on a daily basis so that He can guide and change them. Richard Foster says,

> Picture a narrow ledge with a sheer drop-off on either side. The chasm to the right is the way of moral bankruptcy through human strivings for righteousness. . . . The chasm to the left is the way of moral bankruptcy through the absence of human strivings. . . . On the ledge there is a path, the disciplines of the spiritual life. This path leads to the inner transformation and healing for which we seek. We must never veer off to the right or the left, but stay on the path. . . . As we travel on this path, the blessing of God will come upon us and will reconstruct us into the image of His Son Jesus Christ. We must always remember that the path does not produce the change; it only puts us in the place where the change can occur. This is the way of disciplined grace.[1]

How to Help Your Son Have a Quiet Time and Know the Word

I have a friend who stayed with me for a couple of weeks. One night, it was late, and I noticed that the light was on in the bedroom where he was staying. When I opened the door to see if everything was okay, I found my friend kneeling by his bed, Bible open, head bowed and obviously praying. The sight of him having a quiet time with the Lord made his testimony all the more real to me. Catching him off-guard, as we say, and hearing his barely audible prayers before God convinced me that his professed faith was more than belief; and seeing him humbled before the Lord that night impacted my life forever.

Now, I'm not saying that we should have a quiet time just to impress our sons, or hope someone will discover us on our knees before God. But to expect our sons to have a consistent devotional life when we don't is ludicrous. As in other areas, modeling the right behavior gives our words their "certificate of authenticity."

There is nothing like a personal demonstration by Dad. And you're "it." In Andrew Murray's book *How to Raise Your Children for Christ,* he simply says:

> Not in what we say and teach, but in what we *are* and *do,* lies the power of training. Not as we *think* of an ideal for training our children, but as we *live* do we train them. It is not our wishes or our theory, but our will and our practice that really train. It is by living the Christ-life that we prove that we love it, that we have it; and thus will influence the young mind to love it and to have it, too.[2]

You can have incredible spiritual influence on your son by setting aside a half hour each morning for a quiet time. Have available a Bible, notebook, and prayer list. The whole idea here is to start each day focused on Christ, as one of His disciples. By keeping this daily appointment with God, you demonstrate your commitment to do His will over your own. This will be a wordless sermon to your son about your dependency on Christ and your desire to trust in Him throughout the day.

During your quiet time, allow God to speak to you through His Word. Remember 2 Timothy 3:16–17: "All Scripture is God-breathed and is useful for teaching, rebuking, correcting and training in righteousness, so that the man of God may be thoroughly equipped for every good work." Let all four areas—teaching, rebuking, correcting, and training—become regular key points of Holy Spirit–led introspection and self-examination.

Remind yourself that your appointment is with God, not just to study the Bible or to be able to say, "I had my daily devotional time." Therefore, use the Bible as a tool to encounter Christ and to understand the power of His rising from the grave. That power is available to you, too. That's right. The same power that raised Jesus from the dead will be yours if you come into the presence of God on a daily basis and reflect or meditate on the Word with a view to applying it to your own life. Take time, then, to draw a parallel between what you are reading and how it relates to specific needs you may have in your life—that's why having a notebook is so important.

Date each entry. Record the Scripture passage read. Meditate and write down what God is saying to you in these areas of teachings for your life; exposure of any hidden sin, correction of life's course—that is, moving 180 degrees in the opposite direction from the revealed and confessed sin; training or right living with God, self, and others—that is, putting the Christian life into practice in all your relationships. And, above all, pray about it—again and again. Tell God how you intend to live differently with His power to thoroughly equip you for every good work.

As this process becomes a regular part of your life, invite your son to join you—but not before. Let him see how it is done. Feel what it's like. And experience God with you as together you read passages like 1 Timothy 2:1–8. Then ask, "Are we living peaceful and quiet lives in all godliness and holiness?" "In what ways can we be pleasing to God?" "What does it mean to come to a knowledge of the truth?" and "Are we lifting up holy hands in prayer, without anger or disputing?"

How to Help Your Son Pray

> He who rushes from his bed to his business
>   and waiteth not to worship in prayer,
> Is as foolish as though he had not
>   put on his clothes or washed his face,
> And is as unwise as though
>   he dashed into battle without arms or armor.
>   —Anonymous

The fact that the apostles came to Jesus and asked, "Teach us to pray" (Luke 11:1), tells us that Christ's prayers were different from their prayers. They had heard His prayers. And they knew that to be often alone with God was His secret to a powerful devotional life. No doubt they wanted the same devotion to characterize their lives, and their only hope was to learn to pray like Jesus prayed. The same will be true of our sons.

If they see us praying, and if they make the same connection the apostles did, our sons may also say, "Dad, teach us to pray." To help you when the time comes, let's consider the "model prayer" given by Jesus to His friends.

One powerful tool is to personalize the Lord's Prayer (Matthew 6:9–13), adapting it to individual needs. This is an invaluable thing to pass on to our sons, and it looks like this:

My Father, who has shown me fatherly love through

_____ .

You have shown my need to be reverent through

_____ .

You have revealed your holiness to me by

_____

_____ .

I became a member of your kingdom on _____

and am ministering in _____

_____

to work for the coming of your kingdom. I need your will

to be done in _____ and commit myself to

doing what you reveal your will to be.

My basic needs today are _____ .

I trust you to supply them, and I will not waste my energy

worrying about them.

I have forgiven _____ and want to for-

give anyone who has wronged me.

I ask you to forgive me for _____ .

Today I face temptations to _____ ,

_____ , and _____ .

I know Satan's power is luring me to do what is wrong.

I trust your much stronger power to lead me away from temp-

tation, and so I commit myself now to follow your leadership.[3]

Men, let's not forget the words of Christ in Matthew 21:13: "My house will be called a house of prayer." Here Jesus is referring to the temple, but our bodies are Christ's "home" on earth. And prayer reminds us that we are not our own, because we were bought with a price. Teaching our sons to pray will enable them to, likewise, drive out all that distracts them from honoring God with their bodies (see 1 Corinthians 6:20).

Here are some excellent older—but good—resources on prayer for you and your son to read:

1. E. M. Bounds, *Power Through Prayer* (Chicago: Moody Press, 1979).
2. Jack Hayford, *Prayer Is Invading the Impossible* (Plainfield, NJ: Logos, 1977).
3. Wesley Duewel, *Mighty Prevailing Prayer* (Grand Rapids: Zondervan, 1990).

Helping Your Son to Understand and Experience Worship

Praise, worship, and thanksgiving go together as perfectly as an artist's palette. Although we will need to talk about them

81

at times as separate and distinct activities, they are really bound together in that one and never-changing purpose of drawing us close to the God of all the universe. What is worship, anyway? We could talk about it in theological terms, but we might miss the whole point and focus of worship—like I once did.

Many years ago, when we were at church for a midweek service, our praise leader helped to focus us away from our world and onto the supernatural kingdom of Christ. Then I got up to speak to the congregation.

About one minute into my talk, my son, Patrick—then only eight years old—got up from the last pew on the left side of the auditorium and walked forward. Quietly, he sat down directly in front of me on the first pew. Our eyes met briefly, and we smiled at each other. I was pleased he wanted to be so close. A few more minutes passed, then Patrick got up and walked toward me, right up to the podium where I was standing.

He startled me a bit. *What's he doing?* I thought. But not wanting to miss a beat—I felt I was on a roll—I simply let him stand next to me. In another second he wrapped his little arms around my waist. A tad bit embarrassed, I wrapped one arm around his shoulder. He wasn't going away. In a moment, I looked down and asked in a whisper, "What is it, son?"

"I just need to be near you," he said, squeezing me more tightly now.

That's nice, I thought. Not wanting to disrupt my lesson, I sent him back to his seat. And as he was going, looking dejected, I realized the opportunity I had missed. While I was busy talking about God, a son had wanted to be close to his daddy. *This* father, too preoccupied with a theological thought, had sent his son back to an empty pew. Why hadn't I dropped everything and taught the lesson God was trying to teach me—that worship is nothing other than wanting to embrace, and to be embraced by, the Father who is loving in all His ways.

Patrick—totally unconcerned with an entire congregation looking on—braved the long, lonely walk to the front of the auditorium to be *near me*.

Dads, it is simple enough to make our sons aware of God's longing for them, His children; simple enough to tell them of Christ's compassion for them; simple enough to be available to receive them with open hearts and open arms.

Later, I asked Patrick to forgive me. Even in my failure, I could tell him that God desires his adoration and will never turn him away—never! God would stop. He would turn to my son no matter what was happening in heaven. And He would receive Patrick's whispers of love and his deeply personal need to be near Him.

That day, my son reminded me that longing for me is what worshiping God is all about. If we teach our sons that worship is all-out love for God—the way some men worship sports or hunting or business—they will understand that worship is not a fifteen-minute ritual in church. In our congregation, we usually have a "call to worship" before the actual morning service begins. The more I understand worship, however, the more convinced I am that we should have the "call to worship" at the end of the service—to help people understand that our call to worship Him is the call to love and cling to Him all week long, Sunday to Sunday.

Helping Them Enter In

To help our sons enter into worship, we can introduce them to praise and thanksgiving. Praise worships God for who He is, and thanksgiving worships God for what He has done. And so, it is important that we help our sons discover the attributes and character of God, as well as His actions in real human events.

One way to do this is to study God's Word with our sons. Unlike our daily devotional time—which is meant to be brief and for the purpose of examining ourselves—studying God's Word should be a weekly activity that involves a little more time. Each week, set aside an hour to study the nature and character of God.

Help your son understand that God is holy. God is transcendent. God is eternal. God is intimate. God is Creator—to name but a few of His attributes. You might also study with your son the character and nature of Jesus Christ; after that, the character and nature of the Holy Spirit. Although you may want to involve your pastor to help you choose a study and identify some helpful resources, *you*—and no one else—should lead the study.

Another part of helping your son worship God will be to teach him that daily prayer is a way of life. We've already talked a little about confession as the God-ordained way to forgiveness. Asking God to meet our needs, on the other hand, is a form of worship where we make our requests known before God. In all things, we teach our sons to trust God, no matter what His reply to our prayers may be. Ultimately, we are teaching our sons to submit to God's will.

For in the final analysis, worship is total submission to God. Not slavish, degraded submission—but turning over every aspect of our being to be lifted and changed by God. "If worship does not change us," says Richard Foster, "it has not been worship. To stand before the Holy One of eternity is to change. . . . In worship, an increased power steals its way into the heart's sanctuary, an increased compassion grows in the soul."[4]

This is the kind of living worship we want for our sons.

Helping Your Sons to Make Spiritual Fellowship a Way of Life

Our sons cannot go it alone. Like us, they will need fellowship with other men to master the skills of living—especially spiritual living skills like prayer, worship, confession, and knowledge of the Word. There is great truth to the old saying, "Temptation plus isolation produces sin." By contrast, God says, "As iron sharpens iron, so one man sharpens another" (Proverbs 27:17). Many years ago, when I wrote *Home from Oz*, I had recently learned the significance of fellowship as a key to healthy accountability:

> We can't make it alone. A vital part of the Christian message is that we're not meant to. We need each other! In community, joys are doubled and fears are cut in half. Wisdom is increased and strength is multiplied. My hands become your hands, so our labor is shared. My legs become your legs, so we do not walk alone. This is community in which God says, "Two are better than one. . . . If one falls down, his friend can help him up. . . . If two lie

down together, they will keep warm. . . . Though one be overpowered, two can defend themselves" (Ecclesiastes 4:9–12). The conclusion of the matter is that "A cord of three strands is not quickly broken!"[5]

Now, obviously there are several kinds of fellowship. Some of the most popular forms are small-group and corporate fellowship (like church on Sunday morning). I don't want to end this chapter preaching about "not forsaking the assembly"— although that's important. Suffice it to say, we dads have got to be more open to having fellowship—especially fellowship with other men—if we expect our sons to follow suit.

In a small group of committed Christians, you can learn to care and be cared for, as you share all your struggles in life; you can find encouragement in tough times and a go-get-'em enthusiasm for the goals you're trying to reach; you can find a shared "wisdom" and perspective about life, love, work, money, etc., that is hard to come by in this transient world. We don't want our sons to grow up to be loners, outcasts in this tough society. We want them to find fellowship with like-minded people who share their deepest core value: to honor God with their whole lives.

Therefore, in the next chapter we will talk about how we can help our sons choose the right friends who can "bear one another's burdens," as Paul writes to the Galatians, "and to build each other up in relationship with the Lord."

For Thought and Discussion

1. List ways your relationship with your father influenced your decision to become a Christian. Did it hinder

your decision? Did it influence your perception of God?

2. What is the biggest roadblock in your attempts to guide your son spiritually?

3. The Bible encourages us to "bring [our son] up in the training and instruction of the Lord" (Ephesians 6:4). What does that mean?

7

Bad Company
Corrupts Good Morals

*Helping Your Son to Choose
the Right Friends*

The '90s hit show *Friends* had TV audiences all over America talking about the value of friendships. Keep in mind that the characters portrayed on *Friends* displayed morals that left much to be desired, but their camaraderie did point out the fact that friends help give meaning to your life. And no wonder, since God himself declared, "It is not good for man to be alone."

The problem for all of us is finding *good* friends. The book of Proverbs says a lot about would-be good friends. "A friend loves at all times (17:17)," writes King Solomon, and "a friend . . . sticks closer than a brother" (18:24). He reminds us that "wounds from a friend can be trusted" (27:6)—that is, it may hurt when a friend tells you the truth about yourself, but it's better than flattery from a stranger. Yes, a good friend is one who gets close. And closeness sometimes hurts.

How can we teach our sons about good, strong friendships unless we are willing to take some risks?

One friend who taught me about the joys and risks of friendship is Joel. I first met him in the fall of 1970. We were just kids attending the same junior high. But I think it was providential that our paths should cross—he was likable, and I needed desperately to be liked. I was the proverbial new kid on the block. My parents had recently divorced, and I had moved with my mother to another part of town. The change of location meant a change of schools. The good news was, I met Joel.

Joel was strong, had a great voice, and everyone loved to hear him sing and play guitar. Joel's father had abandoned his family, and he lived in a small townhouse with his mother. His older brothers had moved out years earlier. I recall that Joel was more mature than most boys his age, and his good nature and friendly manner won him many friends. I was thankful he chose me to be one of them.

Joel and his mother were faithful Anglicans, and he often volunteered as an acolyte for Sunday services. At his invitation, I visited Christ Church with him and his mom on Christmas Eve. It was just past midnight and the whole congregation was singing. As I looked around, I could spot a few like me who didn't know quite when to stand or when to kneel, and who crossed themselves in the wrong direction. Joel winked and rolled his eyes in good humor to ease my embarrassment—and after that Christmas Eve, we were inseparable buddies.

Eventually, Joel and I grew up, married, and settled down, but we remained as close as brothers. Fresh out of seminary, I even performed his wedding. Children soon followed, and it seemed for a time that life would be as great to Joel as I thought he deserved. Until I received the phone call.

It was many years ago, just before New Year's, when Joel contacted me. He'd just come home from an emergency room visit where the attending physician had made the discovery. Joel had cancer—inoperable. For over an hour I listened to all the horrible details of the prognosis.

Joel fought courageously for a few months, but all too soon his mother called to say that Joel was near death and needed me to come immediately.

I flew to Florida, where he lived, arriving at his home as quickly as possible. Dustin, his wonderful, heroic wife, was at his side. Joel was awake but very quiet. I took his hand and, overcoming male reserve, I bent down and took Joel in my arms. I kissed his bare head, pressing my cheek against his.

"I like that," he said.

Those were his last words to me.

The next day Joel died, his wife and me by his side. Earlier, the parish priest had gone home. But he asked, in the event Joel passed away, that I perform the pastoral office of Ministration at the Time of Death. I agreed to do so—never expecting to hear myself say, "Into your hands, O merciful Savior, we commend your servant Joel. . . ." My tears and inexpressible anguish made my role difficult to bear, but I was determined to do justice to the litany that Joel loved, for his sake.

Helping to conduct his funeral days later was not any easier. It was just as painful as when, years before, I'd held my infant daughter in my hands as she died. So wounded was I by Joel's premature departure, that writing about helping your sons develop the right kinds of friendships is a *bittersweet* pill to swallow. Sweet is the friendship—like that of Jonathan and David—that rises above all other obligations and sentiments, but bitter, too, when hard circumstances take that friendship away.

How thankful I am to know that, in Christ, Joel and I will meet again one day.

A Father's Friends

I wanted to tell you about Joel because I believe that the quality of our friendships can be the perfect foundation to help our sons choose the right relationships later in life. In this day of fair-weather friends, we want our sons to see in our relationships—especially man-to-man relationships—friends who stick together in adversity, give more than they expect to receive, and who daily encourage each other to faithfulness, love, and service to God.

My close friends have been models for my son in these areas. There was Bruce, my brother-in-law, who was a worship leader for our church. He gave countless, selfless hours helping me with home repair and car maintenance. Paul, a leader with our church, regularly watched our children, freeing Rachel and me to have some much-needed breaks. Kevin, a fellow presbyter, brought encouraging audiotapes of sermons and wonderful Christ-centered books for us to read. And there was Phil, always eager to lend a helping hand.

These incredible, armor-bearing brothers were living, tangible examples of the kind of friends I prayed my son would one day choose, and I also prayed that they represented the kind of friend he would one day become.

This is why bringing our sons into the company of men is so important. It shows them what to look for and to know how masculine friendship feels—even when we can't put it into words. Also, it helps our sons experience male camaraderie with all of its nuances, like strong handshakes, slaps on the back, deep voices, and the smell of sweat and toil. Unfortunately, friendships among men can be, and often are, quite rare these days. Men simply don't have the kind of friendships women seem to take for granted.

Because men are territorial—that is, we like to set geographical boundaries much like dogs create with their scent—we often find closeness with other men difficult to achieve. Closeness feels awkward. We're a bit suspicious. Like dogs, our body language often says, in a not-so-subtle way, "If you get too close, I'll either run away or bite." Women, on the other hand, seem less concerned with maintaining distance. They have an extraordinary giftedness for intimacy.

Yes, there is a lot to be wary of in this world. But when we dads model friendship for our sons, we show them how to come into the company of men for encouragement and affirmation, and to express themselves freely. When we allow our sons to watch our friendships, they will get to witness, firsthand, what men with spiritual values talk about and how they treat each other, their wives, and their children.

Occasionally—say, when a friend stops by for coffee, or you go to help him put up a fence—why not let your son tag along? This can have more benefit than a canned, once-a-year father/son outing at the ballpark. It brings your son into your world and the world of male companionship. There's so little of this in our isolating society, yet it's crucial for a boy as he develops a healthy male identity.

You can even teach your son a lot by bringing him into the company of men who don't necessarily share your spiritual values. If you are a committed Christian yourself, you can easily make the distinction for your son between a spiritual friendship and a "reconciling friendship." Some of the men you know will be fellow Christians, and some will be guys whom you want to influence for their good—hoping to lead them back to church and into reconciliation with God.

Just as it's important that our sons be allowed to observe our world, it's important to observe their world, too, to be concerned about the "territory" in which they live, and to show it. Lots of men grow up feeling ripped off, saying, "My parents couldn't have cared less who my friends were, or where we hung out." They still carry the sting of their dads' unconcern and abandonment. Take the time and responsibility to be aware of and to monitor who your son spends time with—whether it's on a ball field or a local playground or just around the neighborhood. Find a good reason to visit the homes of your son's friends and meet their parents. It's better to form this habit when your children are young—so start early. You will never lose by showing a heartfelt interest in your son's world!

Helping Our Sons Watch Out for Manipulative "Friends"

The best friendships are full of give-and-take; they learn from each other and they offer a good, positive challenge to be better at a skill or a sport. Of course, our sons will encounter some boys who are not so good for them. There are some so-called friends we should warn our sons about. In his book *Man, the Manipulator,* Everett Shostrom gives us a good look at some of the major traits of manipulative relationships.[1]

The Dictator. This is the kid who dominates and controls people by ordering them around. In relating to others, he often projects a parent or boss image. As a father, I had to remind Patrick that we, his parents, were the only ones who had the authority to tell him what to do—not his friends. We had taught him to come home or call us if he had any doubts or suspicions about anything a friend was telling him to do. Basically, we helped him to trust his instincts. If something doesn't feel right, we told him that he had our permission to just leave or to phone us immediately.

The Weakling. This is the boy who likes to be dominated and relates to people in a way that makes everyone else re-sponsible for his problems and failures. This person may also elicit sympathy and solace from his friends by playing the martyr in the relationship. He tries to get people to feel sorry for him. If your son finds himself sought out by a boy like this, I'd recommend that he refer his friend to a counselor at school or to a youth minister at church. Also, make it plain to your son that his friend should be the one responsible to get the help he needs to manage his personal struggles.

The Calculator. This boy controls others by deceiving, lying, and outwitting people. As he grows older he can be-come seductive or the high-pressure salesperson or con artist we all avoid. We need to encourage our sons to stay alert to subtle inconsistencies or exaggerations in the stories a friend tells him. I would tell Patrick that if he caught a friend telling a lie, he was to confront him and explain that he was only allowed to hang out with guys who told the truth. Lying was strictly prohibited in our house, and Patrick knew that he would be severely disciplined for being deceitful.

The Clinging Vine. This boy is dependent upon others and relates to them like the "perpetual child," the "hypochondriac," the "attention demander," or the "helpless one." As with the weakling friend, I'd urge you to tell your son to have his friend seek professional help from an experienced counselor or clergyman. I'd also limit the amount of time your son spends with such a friend. It's all right to be helpful—but to be put into the role of surrogate parent or "savior" is dangerous and unnecessary.

The Bully. This guy controls friends through hostility and cruelty and relates to them with constant put-downs, sarcasm, and even the threat of physical abuse. Patrick was not allowed to be around such a kid. It was that simple. He was taught to just walk away. If that didn't work and he had been physically threatened, he was told to go get help from either his teacher or one of the school administrators. As a last resort, he was trained (and had our permission) to punch the boy one time, hard in the nose or in the gut and to just get out of there. Not on school grounds, of course. It was risky business, I know—but we didn't want to be overprotective of our son, and neither did we want to encourage him to use violence as a means for solving every problem. One father I know has his son and the "bully" go to the local YMCA and duke it out in a legitimate boxing ring, with boxing gloves and a referee. He tells me it's worked out pretty well—so far.

The Nice Guy. This boy exaggerates caring and love and relates to people on a very superficial level by pleasing everyone and always saying what he thinks others want to hear. We told Patrick that real friends aren't afraid to tell you what they think or how they're feeling. We also explained to him that speaking to a friend honestly is not a license for being intentionally hurtful in the things we say. Friendships, we told him, should have a balance of constructive criticism and tolerance.

The Judge. This person dominates people by being extremely critical and comparing them with others, and specializes in making people feel ashamed and guilty. We told Patrick that only God is Judge. No one can see into a man's heart except the Almighty. We told him to compare himself only to Jesus. And we would remind him that it was our Lord who nailed both guilt and shame to the cross. We also explained to Patrick that people who are overly critical and judgmental often don't like themselves. They are to be encouraged, we told him, because they likely came from homes where there was little love or forgiveness and probably no leeway for imperfection.

Shostrom says that, by contrast, our sons should seek out relationships characterized by *honesty, awareness, freedom,* and *trust.* A good friend, he explains, is able to express his feelings, whatever they may be. He will be candid, genuinely himself around his friends. He will listen to others and be honest with himself. He will be spontaneous, free to live up to his potential. A good friend is one who is in control of his own life, and not a puppet or an object of others.

A Friend Close to Home

One final, important thought.

If your wife is not your best friend, work at making your relationship with her better than any other. Because the relationship you and your wife have is the cornerstone upon which your son will build all his friendships, it is vital that he view your relationship as spiritually and emotionally healthy. This means that it is characterized by kindness, thoughtfulness, affection, candidness, and letting God be the Master of your lives. If separation or divorce has already occurred, it is important that you deal with your personal opinions about your estranged or former spouse with another adult, not with your son. Let him hear only the good things you have to say about his mother.

The benefits your son will gain by observing your friendship with your wife will be many. Let me list a few.

First, he will be more likely to choose a better mate—one who has similar interests and is more compatible. Children acquire an idea of what they want in a partner by watching us and examining our marital relationship.

Second, he will have some skills and insight on how to have a successful marriage. Because your marriage has been a model to him, he'll have a better idea of what to expect going into his own marriage. All the things we do well—or not so well—he will likely bring into a relationship of his own.

Lastly, he'll know how to model the same skills and traits for his sons when the time comes.

A Man Who Laid Down His Life for His Friends

Calvin had coal black hair and brown eyes. His slender build made him appear taller than he really was. Still, he was over six feet. He had gone to a university in Texas to be trained as a missionary. Although he was more interested in people than books, he did quite well as a student. And after graduation, his professors suggested he go right on to graduate school.

Needing a break, he decided to take a short missionary trip to South America where he could get some much needed hands-on experience in the field before returning to his studies.

Not one to go it alone, Calvin was joined by his friends Bill, Todd, Dana, and Andrea. All had been students at the same university, and the chance to do missionary work together was something they'd talked about. So they boarded a plane to Brazil, where they would spend three months helping to plant a church.

One month into their stay, tragedy struck. They were swimming together in the Pacific Ocean when a riptide pulled them all out to sea. Calvin, Bill, and Todd made their way back to shore only to discover that Dana and Andrea weren't with them. Without concern for his personal safety, Calvin dove back into the water. He swam to Dana and Andrea and literally pulled them to the edge of the surf where Bill and Todd could easily lift them to safety. But before Calvin could catch his breath, another riptide carried him back out to sea. Exhausted from the rescue, Calvin obviously had no strength left to fight the strong current, and he drowned a few yards from those he'd saved.

Without Calvin's heroic effort, two would have died that day instead of one. Dana's and Andrea's parents spoke at Calvin's memorial service. They spoke of how blessed they were to have had Calvin as a friend to their daughters.

"Had we been there, we would have done everything to save the lives of our children," they said. "But, we weren't there. And God appointed Calvin to be their rescuer. He laid down his life for his friends."

For Thought and Discussion

1. What would you tell your son to do if he encountered a bully? Would you encourage your son to resort to physical retaliation if threatened with bodily harm?

2. Do you think it's a good idea to let our sons learn martial arts for the purpose of self-defense? What about the opinion that karate is part of a pagan religion?

3. Do you know or can you quickly get a hold of the names, addresses, and phone numbers of all your son's closest friends? Have you been to their homes? Have you met their parents?

8

"Ask Not What Your Country Can Do for You . . ."

Helping Your Son to Be a Good Citizen

A commitment to active citizenship has always been an American ideal. Some believe, however, that this commitment is weakening among young people. Part of the problem is that we dads have forgotten to teach our sons that they, like us, have a lifetime obligation as citizens to serve our nation and our communities. Our sons must learn through us to appreciate the importance of their citizenship to the health and preservation of our free and democratic system. They need to know that the contribution they make by charitable giving and voluntary service is part of the greater good, and that when they are good citizens who serve, they personally benefit, as well.

Why Be a "Good Citizen"?

Serving others in the community brings out the best in the server. Time and again my students tell me that when they help others, a side of them emerges that is more patient, more kind, and more giving than they ever thought they could be. "I like that part of myself," they say. It's the side of their personalities that acts in benevolence and goodwill to show them that they are capable of serving others—and that they can like it!

Serving others and being good citizens helps them to live in a better world. And a better world means better living conditions. It's interesting to read what God says through Jeremiah. He gives Israelite families instructions on how to behave as minority citizens living in Babylon: "Seek the peace and prosperity of the city to which I have carried you into exile. Pray to the Lord for it, because if it prospers, you too will prosper" (Jeremiah 29:7). In the place of apathy or even vengeance, God tells the Israelite community to be good and productive citizens, for their own sake as well as for the sake of the empire!

Being a good citizen also brings respect. When the apostle Paul talks about the qualifications for leaders in the church, he says they must have a good reputation in the community where they live. There is no better way to build a good reputation in a city or town than to be willing to volunteer for community projects, such as Neighborhood Watch, Meals on Wheels, Special Olympics, Boy Scouts, or coaching a sports team. Serving the neighborhood and exercising good citizenship prepares our sons to be future leaders of the church.

There is, however, a religious movement that seeks a finer life for all Americans to the neglect of evangelism and the supernatural ability of God to make our world better. Carl F. H. Henry, former editor of *Christianity Today,* makes the point that we need to be careful and not be overly reliant on our government for all the solutions to life's problems. Although the world may find the gospel of Jesus Christ too simple an answer to presumably unsolvable social problems, our sons should be taught the importance of the Holy Spirit's transforming power.[1]

The answer, according to Henry, is balance. He concludes that Christianity does have a vital stake in our government but warns that it "dare not forget nor let the world forget— that what the social order most needs is a new race of men— men equipped not simply with textbooks and new laws but with new hearts."

"Paul [the apostle] presents a greater vision still," writes John R. Stott in his book *God's New Society.*[2] In Paul's letter to the Ephesians, he "sees the human predicament as something deeper than the injustice of the economic structure and so propounds a yet more radical solution. He writes of nothing less than a 'new creation.'"

It is my belief that the best way to prepare your son to be a good citizen is to help him be a good citizen of the kingdom of God. What our world needs most is the message of Ephesians with its emphasis on a new kingdom. Membership in this kingdom of God is characterized by valuing life in the place of death; by unity and reconciliation in the place of alienation and division; by the wholesome standards of righteousness in the place of corruption and wickedness; by love and peace in the place of hatred and strife; and by "unremitting conflict with evil in the place of a flabby compromise with it," as Stott puts it.

When Rodney King asked, after the Los Angeles riots, "Can we all get along?" I thought, *the answer from a worldly point of view is no.* Only in God's kingdom do we find the theme of uniting all things in Christ. Only among God's citizens is there a breaking down of all that separates us from God—all that separates one ethnic group from another, husband from wife, parent from child. Let's teach our sons the vision of a renewed community—to live out the conviction that as the church goes, so goes the nation!

Helping Our Sons Pray for Our Nation

The Bible states, "If my people, who are called by name, will humble themselves and pray and seek my face and turn from their wicked ways, then will I hear from heaven and will forgive their sin and will heal their land" (2 Chronicles 7:14). We dads can model and teach our sons to pray daily for our land to be healed. For starters, ask your son to join you in praying for:

- authorities and key officials
- major legislations being debated
- legal battles that will affect the laws of the land
- the morals of those in authority—that they be awakened to the laws of God written on their hearts!

Also pray that God will direct our leaders to walk in the paths of righteousness so that He may preserve the peace of the nation and the safety of all. Pray also for our cities that are rampant with crime, for families in our neighborhoods that are breaking up, for children who are being destroyed by drugs, pornography, abortion. Read Psalm 119:147: "I rise before dawn and cry for help." Encourage your son to be a person who intercedes for the salvation of all people.

Teaching Our Sons Good Citizenship

Here are some suggestions for teaching good citizenship. Using Thomas Jefferson's magnificent words found in our country's *Declaration of Independence,* examine with your son every citizen's "unalienable rights": life, liberty, and the pursuit of happiness.

Right to life. Teach your son that all human life is sacred, by virtue of being created in the image of God (Genesis 1:27). Help him memorize Exodus 20:13: "Thou shalt not kill" (KJV). Explain to him that all forms of "life-stealing"— murder, suicide, abortion, and euthanasia—are sins in the eyes of God. Teach him to respect our physical environment and all of the earth's inhabitants, that he is to be a guardian and caretaker of God's creation.

Right to liberty. Teach your son that all human beings "are endowed by their Creator" with equal dignity and worth and are entitled to civil liberty under God's law. Read to him Colossians 3:11: "Here there is no Greek or Jew, circumcised or uncircumcised, barbarian, Scythian, slave or free, but Christ is all, and is in all," and Galatians 3:28: "There is neither Jew nor Greek, slave nor free, male nor female, for you are all one in Christ Jesus." Reflect with him on the words of Dr. Martin

Luther King Jr.: "We must learn to live together as brothers or perish together as fools." Teach your son to be grateful to Jesus Christ who, according to Scripture, proclaims freedom to the prisoner and gives release to the oppressed (see Luke 4:18).

Right to pursue happiness. Real happiness is the contentment that comes from a morally good life (see Matthew 5:6). Read with your son Ecclesiastes 3:12 and 12:13. Put together, they read, "I know that there is nothing better for men than to be happy and do good while they live. . . . Now all has been heard; here is the conclusion of the matter: Fear God and keep his commandments, for this is the whole duty of man."

Help to develop your son's spirit of volunteerism. There is an amazing array of volunteer activities that, in the opinion of participants, literally changes lives. One group of young men and women went to a Sioux reservation in South Dakota to do painting, tiling, and carpentry at a YMCA. Another group traveled to Juarez, Mexico, to help build a *serviglesia*, a church to serve the poor. Ten or more young people headed for Appalachia's "Valley of Despair" to plant trees and work on construction and furniture-building projects.

Other volunteer activities have included painting an elementary school gym in East Menlo Park, California. In Boston, older teens tend to homeless women every night at Rosie's Place, a local shelter. In Evanston, Illinois, young volunteers have started an "adopt a grandparent" program to aid the elderly. And in Ann Arbor, Michigan, students from the University of Michigan help low-income citizens with their tax returns. These volunteer services are similar to the work of Habitat for Humanity, another worthy cause.

Obviously, many of the volunteer activities mentioned above are for the older teen and are supervised by adults. But there are many local, less dependent activities, such as volunteering to walk the dog for elderly neighbors, mowing lawns and doing light housework for a widow, or collecting used toys (in good condition) for low-income families.

I also recommend reading the local newspaper or watching the evening news with your son. Discuss regional, national, and global events. Once a week you could hold a dinnertime discussion (not a lecture) about a social, legal, or political problem. Ask your son what he thinks.

Fathers can model volunteerism while spending time with their sons by coaching or refereeing their child's soccer team, baseball team, or basketball team; help out with practice, or be a team manager. If you can't coach, another idea would be to volunteer with your son at a food bank or clothing consignment store. Volunteer to help with maintenance at a shelter or crisis pregnancy center. Try becoming a Scout leader.

The sky's the limit. The important thing is that you and your son do it together. Whatever you choose to do, the best thing you can spend on your son is time! Your time. And the best way to pass on a sense of honor and citizenship is to show your son what you value. If you value your community and your nation, so will he.

For Thought and Discussion

1. Paul the apostle writes, "Everyone must submit himself to the governing authorities, for there is no authority

except that which God has established" (Romans 13:1). First Peter 2:13 states, "Submit yourselves for the Lord's sake to every authority instituted among men." Discuss what these mean.

2. What would you tell your son to do if the government asked him to do something that violated his conscience? Refer to Acts 5:29.

3. Do you think being a good citizen involves voting in local and national elections? Serving in the military? Entering politics and playing a part in the government of the country? Discuss.

9

The Birds and the Bees

Helping Your Son to Understand His Sexuality and to Prepare for Marriage

Most boys, if they looked at the table of contents, would probably turn to this chapter first!

If we are really going to help our sons become well-adjusted and informed about their sexuality, we need to talk with them at a level that's deeper than an analysis of a young man's sexual pressures.

I want to provide fundamental understanding of male sexuality and some insights on how to prepare your son for one of the most important decisions of his life—choosing a marriage partner. Helping your son control his sexual appetite before marriage, in this day and age, is a great accomplishment. The key, however, is not found in limiting your son's knowledge about sex—quite the opposite. The more your son knows and understands of human sexuality, the more likely he will be to keep his sexuality in perspective, and the more likely he will be to save sexual intimacy until marriage.

As a former president of an Episcopal, classical academy, it was not unusual to hear my elementary school boys and girls say to each other, "Hey, that's a really sexy outfit!" *Sexy?* I wonder. Where do children—who can't be ten yet—get the term *sexy?* More important, how do they learn to equate *sexy* with things we wear? We know the answer. The treatment of human sexuality in the advertising media is often linked with selling products. TV, movies, and the printed page can be and often are sources of sexual innuendoes, distortions, and outright deception.

If we don't talk to our sons about their awakening sexuality, who will? Where do you want your son's sexual identity, knowledge, and attitudes to come from?

Your Son's Sexual Identity

You can probably remember with me when we were young and some of the guys viewed sexual knowledge as a litmus test of acceptability. As early as the fourth grade I was grilled by some older guy with questions about a girl's reproductive organs. I would literally sweat it out as he talked about things of which I had no clue. Just being approached like that allowed me to be "one of the guys"—at least until the next time.

Being included in this kind of discussion became a source of identity for me. It told me in ways I could understand that I was male, that I was acceptable as a boy among boys. Unfortunately, the proof of admissibility only got more intense, and the requirements more difficult to meet as I reached the teen years. In our high school, sexual intercourse was the sole criteria for adulthood and a way of proclaiming to our peer group that we were not homosexual. I was even accused of being homosexual because I'd chosen a path of abstinence. I had made a commitment to Christ at age fifteen, and I wanted to live in a way that was acceptable to God. Losing my virginity was not an option to me.

Unfortunately, college presented a huge challenge. (And I was at a Christian school!) My girlfriend began to pressure me about sex. She said it was her way of feeling secure and fulfilling her desire to be needed, to belong. Now there were two of us who had deep, gnawing questions regarding our personal identity. It's not difficult to see how things heated up between us, and if it hadn't been for my transfer to another school, it's likely she would have become pregnant.

As a man, you will impact your son's personal identity more than anyone else besides his mother. All young people are, consciously or unconsciously, trying to find out who they are, where they are going, and generally what life is about— including sexual identity. Our sons struggle with what society expects of them. Some are even getting involved in sex for largely nonsexual reasons. They are looking for the act of sex to affirm, approve, or give meaning to their lives. Their sexual experience becomes an endless search for intimacy—something that may have eluded them while they were growing up. Here's a case in point taken from the syndicated column of Dr. Schwarzbeck called "Children Today."[1]

Sexually Active Teens Often Seeking "Special" Person

Alexa, an attractive sixteen-year-old, looked down at the floor. Circles under her reddened eyes told much of her story.

"I've been sexually active since last year," she said. "I'm not pregnant. I'm not into drugs, nothing like that, but I'm getting pretty messed up."

She explained that she feared losing her boyfriend, whom she especially liked because "he understands me." A year earlier she had a similar experience with another boy she felt comfortable talking to.

"I know the big thing is sex, but that's really not it," she said. "I'm sad and I'm desperate. I need one special person who I can go to when it's hard for me. I'd do anything to have that."

Alexa, crying, explained that, "It was me that got our sexual thing going. As we got to know each other, I felt like I had to feel worthwhile. I had to give him something special. He didn't say he would leave me . . . but I started to worry about that."

"I get along easier with boys," she said. "Boys have been my best friends. I keep thinking, *When will I find that one special person who I can always go to?*"

Her dream is to find another youngster who will give her available, sensitive parenting. Sex is a front that makes her longing seem grown-up, rather than an expression of unmet early childhood needs.

As we listen carefully to Alexa, we hear a girl who—much like our sons—is searching for a source of consistent affection that is missing in her life. When she seeks out "a special person" to make her feel valued and loved, she has in essence turned to the opposite sex and sexual intercourse for proof. That proof, however, should come from you, Dad! You need to be that "special person" your son can always go to.

Another story comes to mind.

I had been a guest speaker for a large church in Atlanta. My message that Sunday was "Turning the Hearts of Fathers Toward Home," and I concluded with a deeply moving story I'd once heard:

There was a young father who, early on a Saturday morning, was awakened by his three children. They wanted to go to the park just across the street to build a fort in the wooded area just past the playground. Knowing they would need his approval and help they had begun to jump up and down on his bed shouting, "Dad, let's build the fort!"

"I have to go in to work today," was the disappointing reply. "But next Saturday, we'll build the fort, okay?"

"Okay, Dad," the kids agreed.

Next Saturday came, but the kids were not taking any chances. To make sure their father would not forget his promise they again burst into his bedroom, but this time they brought with them a hammer, nails, and wood. Jumping on the bed they began to shout aloud, "Dad, let's build the fort!"

"Oh, I'm so sorry kids. . . . I forgot all about it, and I've got to go into work," said the ambitious father, now wiping the sleep from his eyes. As his youngest began to weep the father added, "But next week, I'll take off. I promise. We'll build the fort, you'll see!"

Finally the succeeding Saturday came. The young father and his three children were now breakfasting together. At their feet lay the hammer, the nails and wood to build the fort. They were almost at the front door when the phone rang. All three children stood motionless waiting to see what their dad would do. Finally the young father could stand it no more. He quickly walked to the phone and picked it up. On the other end was his boss.

"Bill," said the boss, "I need you to come in this morning. You are the only one who can close this deal."

What do I do? agonized the young father. *I don't want to disappoint my kids, but I certainly don't want to disappoint my boss. I guess it's a choice between my career or my kids.*

"I know what, kids," the father began slowly, "I've got to go into work today, but I won't be long. You start building the fort without me and then I'll come home and put on the finishing touches."

The children reluctantly agreed and headed across the street to start building the fort. About a half hour had passed and the youngest child, arms filled with wood, was trying to cross the busy street in front of their house when he was struck by an automobile and killed.

The young father now sat at the interment of his young son. Not being able to contain himself any longer, he stood to his feet, tears pouring down his cheeks. Slowly, he began to speak to the fathers who were in attendance that day, including his boss.

"Men, if I could leave you one piece of advice today it would be this: Build the fort today, dads, please build the fort today!"

After I had ended my message with this powerful illustration, dozens of men came forward. One in particular caught my attention with the words, "I'm a homosexual; I know I've been searching for my father in illicit sexual relationships with men." I hugged him as he wept. The experience was for me a profound revelation. It lent credibility to the scientific studies that tell us that the more nurturing the father, the more masculine the son.

If you want to impact your son's personal sense of well-being and help him build a strong masculine and sexual identity, here are some things you can do:

Expect the best. A prominent Harvard University psychologist, Dr. R. Rosenthal, established a link between how we regard or think about an individual and the behavior or performance of that individual. Labeled the *Pygmalion Effect*, Rosenthal says that this powerful phenomenon can be both negative as well as positive in its impact.[2]

My friend and colleague, Dr. R. Dale Fike, once said that if fathers can come to understand the importance of setting positive expectations for their sons and can practice a positive mental attitude of expecting them to be successful, well-adjusted, and masculine adults, then it is highly likely they will grow up to have a strong personal and sexual identity.

Embrace your son. Touching (e.g., holding, rocking, cuddling, physical playing, a squeeze on the arm, an arm around the shoulder, etc.) is linked with many psychological and physiological benefits. The point is that you are "embracing" your son as a human being, affirming him as a man. We dads have to learn the importance of touch to our son's life-span development. If you grew up with a physically distant father yourself, don't repeat the cycle. Learn from your wife or men you know to be affectionate with their children. Don't let your son grow up experiencing the same lack of touch you did. Vow to break the cycle today!

Be involved. In my work as executive director with the Southwest Center for Fathering, involvement—as a fathering technique—was high on our list of priorities for dads to practice. Dr. Urie Bronfenbrenner, a leading developmental psychologist, suggests that when fathers are not involved, they contribute to their son's low motivation for achievement, their inability to defer immediate rewards for later benefits, low self-esteem, greater susceptibility to peer pressure, and juvenile delinquency.

To help prevent this, start when your son is an infant—be part of his feeding schedule (hold the bottle, wipe his chin, burp him), change his diapers and clothing on a regular basis, help put him to bed, read him bedtime stories, pray with him, and bless him (reciting words of praise over his head with your hand on his body). I strongly recommend the bestselling book *The Blessing* by Gary Smalley and John Trent.[3]

As your boy gets older, think about rearranging your work schedule or changing jobs. This will not be easy. When Patrick entered first grade, I decided to find a new job. Being a full-time professor and administrator at a university gobbled up huge chunks of time, so I reduced my hours to an adjunct professor and took a position as headmaster at my son's private school. I got to walk him to school, have lunch with him on a regular basis, and give him that focused attention he craved.

Make dinnertime a priority in your household. As your son gets older, he'll get more involved with activities outside the home. To help him reconnect with you, require him to have dinner with you at least four nights a week. Eating a meal together will give you both a chance to talk and find out what's going on in each other's world. You could also include a "Family Night," setting aside one evening each week to be involved in something your son wants to do. Let him dictate the evening's activity—shooting baskets, going to a movie or dinner at a restaurant, watching a DVD or TV program, or taking a walk or jog through the park. Whatever. Just do something together!

Nurture him. According to my friend and colleague Dr. Ken Canfield, nurturance is expressed by attitudes, words, and actions. Nurturance can even be nonverbal, but should include affection (don't forget to speak the language of love to your son, especially the words "I love you!"); support (be there for his athletic events, after-school programs, and any significant religious occasions, such as confirmation and baptism); comfort (tuck him into bed, hold him, rock him, kiss his "boo-boo's"); and intimacy (don't underestimate your actual physical presence; boys tell us that having their fathers in the next room while they sleep is very reassuring to them).

Your Son's Knowledge of Sex

Talking about the birds and the bees to your son is no small task! But it begins long before that heart-to-heart talk between father and son. You teach your son about human sexuality by the way in which you relate to your wife. What he sees will be what he gets in the way of habits, thoughts, feelings, and attitudes. It is truly amazing what children learn by watching us—it is God's plan, His way of preparing our sons for life. Again, the greatest gift a man can give his son is to love his mother! And, I might add, love her in appropriate ways.

In the bestselling book *The Gift of Sex,* Clifford and Joyce Penner point out the powerful role we fathers play in shaping our sons' ideas of how sex should be. They write:

> Father's openness in the expression of his feelings, especially his softer feelings of warmth, care, tenderness,

sadness and hurt, will probably be the example we use in our own understanding of "how men are." As he is able to share the full range of his emotions, he is also able to respond to his wife with the total intensity that makes for a fulfilling sexual life. In homes where the father has difficulty with the expression of his emotions, the children often grow up to have difficulty with a satisfying sexual expression of themselves.

A son, particularly, will model himself after his father. How much did your father feel free to touch you . . . or other family members? How free was he to express his feelings? How willing was he to admit his mistakes? What kind of care and respect did he show for your mother? Was he tentative and unsure in relation to her, or confident and caring? Were you able to sense that he loved her totally, not just as an object of his sexual desire? All of these issues are the threads from which your sexual attitudes are woven.[4]

This is why being consistent and truthful with our actions is so important. If I say to my son, "Sex with your mother is a natural and wonderful part of our marriage," but give off a mixed message when I'm trying to be affectionate with her that "it's really awkward and uncomfortable for us," what is he to believe? Or if you say, "I love your mother," but put her down or ridicule her or, worse, abuse her physically or verbally, how is he to think about the male/female relationship in general? Fathers, we must remember that what our sons bring into their own sexual relationship will largely come from us. Gordon Dalbey says it best:

So many of the problems that often erupt in a marriage can be traced to the husband's "father-wound"—that is, the lack he feels from not having the kind of strong human fathering that God intended. Despite the best of intentions, too many fathers fail to teach their boys how to deal with their own maleness.[5]

There are some sex myths about men that our sons could learn from us if we're not careful:

Men never show their emotions. As dads, we will need to model for our sons that expressing fear, vulnerability, tenderness, and even confusion at times is not a sign of weakness or a lack of masculinity. It is simply being human! We need to encourage our sons to share their emotions—such as feelings of being uptight or reluctant to try new things for fear of looking stupid—with their wives, and to ask for help in knowing how to satisfy them physically.

Sex is the man's charge. We need to let our sons know that initiating sex, or arousing their wife, or even deciding how sex should be done is not always their responsibility. Also, because boys are taught to be competitive at an early age, there is the expectation to perform well. Such an expectation usually backfires: The harder they try to be super studs, the less likely they are to do well. We must teach them that sex between a husband and wife is a shared responsibility.

All touching is the man's license for sex. Many boys are taught at a young age that physical contact between people is either sexual or aggressive. Our culture also teaches boys that touching is unacceptable unless it leads to sex. We need to model for our sons that not all hugging, caressing, and patting is sexual in nature. And that tenderness and sensitivity is what their wives will crave most as a necessary component for all sexual encounters.

It is important to help our sons understand that "petting" and "making out" are part of God's plan for sexual arousal within marriage—making preparation for sexual intercourse between a husband and wife. We taught our son that holding hands, putting your arm around your girlfriend's shoulders, and the proverbial good-night kiss (a peck on the cheek) were the only acceptable forms of dating affection, at least until he had graduated from high school.

Helping Your Son to Understand Himself Sexually

I like the story of the little girl who, when taking a shower with her mother, began to notice the differences between her body and that of her mom's. After the comparison was made, she looked up and asked her mother, "Why am I so plain and you're so fancy?" Don't you just love the innocence of childhood? Don't you wish you could keep them there forever?

As our sons mature, they'll want to know more about their physical appearance. And, in particular, they'll want to know more about their sexual organs and sex.

Give your son a brief sketch of both the male and female anatomy. Don't leave this discussion to the biology or health teacher or textbooks. And most definitely don't leave it to his friends with *Playboy* or *Hustler* magazines. A diagram explaining the various parts of the body would be a very helpful tool as you discuss with your son the beautiful, intricate, and complex structure of the human body. Take it slow and easy. Young children who are not "awakened" sexually by hormone production may just want facts about their anatomy. No doubt your son has been asking questions from the time he was a little boy. In early adolescence, somewhere between eleven and thirteen, when hormones are flowing, give him some more information. And then a few years later, when he's getting interested in relationships with girls, it's time for "the talk." Since parents are the best judges of their children's level of maturity, I'd recommend that you talk to your wife about her perceptions of your son's receptivity and comprehension.

One of the most difficult times for boys is puberty.

As your son's body begins to change at this time, he may become acutely aware of body image and be highly critical of his physical appearance. He will begin to compare his own body with his expectations for body type, the opinions of peers, and relevant adults—especially his father's evaluation and the cultural norms and standards put forth in print, on TV, and in movies. It is important that you affirm your son's awakening body image. Few of us fit the "ideal"—the V-shaped torso, narrow hips, and over-developed muscles. Let him know that he is normal. Share with him how you adjusted to the same general problem of adolescent body image and the mythical body ideal. If chubbiness or skinniness, buck teeth or acne is a problem, be sensitive to his feelings of self-consciousness. This is the time to tell him how you survived similar adolescent anxieties and stresses. Another important point of discussion with your son has to do with genitalia.

Fathers should be aware that the fallacy that the larger a man's penis, the better he will be able to satisfy a woman, can often occupy their son's thoughts. Perpetuated by crude locker room comparisons, your son may question whether or not he is adequately endowed in this area. The truth of the matter is, Masters and Johnson have found that a smaller, un-aroused penis size—when sexually stimulated—enlarges more than a larger, un-aroused penis. Our sons need to know that penis size is approximately the same for all men when erection occurs—and there is no difference in sexual satisfaction.

Many men feel very uncomfortable talking about masturbation. Some men think, *I don't want to signal to my son that this is natural and okay. If he hasn't started, I don't want him to.* I can understand this concern, but to be realistic, we need to know that most boys will do this at some time during adolescence. "It is my opinion," says Dr. James Dobson, "that masturbation is not much of an issue with God." He then gives this advice to teens:

> It's a normal part of adolescence that involves no one else. It does not cause disease, it does not produce babies. . . . I'm not telling you to masturbate, and I hope you won't feel the need for it. But if you do, it is my opinion that you should not struggle with guilt over it.
>
> Why do I tell you this? Because I deal with so many Christian young people who are torn apart with guilt over masturbation; they want to stop and just can't. I would like to help you avoid that agony. The best I can do is suggest that you talk with God personally about this matter and decide what He wants you to do. I'll leave it there between you and Him.[6]

My opinion is similar to Dobson's. A boy in puberty will have strong biological urges. Since intercourse is for marriage, he'll be left with just two options. One will be to rely solely on a "wet dream" to relieve stress. The other will be to masturbate. For better or worse, the Bible is conspicuously silent about the subject. On the other hand, psychologists tell me that there is no relationship between masturbation and later sexual adjustment in marriage.

As Patrick's dad, what I was concerned about was not the actual, physical act of masturbation. Rather, it was the sexual fantasies and lustful thoughts that might accompany it. Therefore, I wanted to talk openly with my son about masturbation as sexual self-stimulation, and at the same time warn him to take every thought captive in Christ. This means that, while I will not prohibit my son's natural and probable tendency to masturbate during adolescence, I will encourage him not to use pornography, sexually explicit films, or, in general, sexual fantasies to induce ejaculation. Believe it or not, a boy can masturbate without the use of sexual fantasy and can even decrease sexual fantasies through the use of self-stimulation.

This is also when dads will want to talk directly about Internet pornography and sexually explicit material of any kind. The critical issue for sons to understand is the element of *comparison*. When boys use illicit, sexually disconcerting images to induce ejaculation, they are training their young bodies to respond only to that kind of promiscuous trigger—even when later married. Therefore, unsuspecting future wives often are forced to suffer the humiliating indignity of performing sexually in ways that resemble these earlier similes. For some men who have sexually habituated themselves to only respond to pornography, their wife's body may never be enough for natural arousal to occur. Think of how terrible this would be for an otherwise fully satisfying marriage.

This is why pornography of any kind must never be an option, and why fathers must help eliminate the risk of exposure by putting certain safeguards in place—like blocking pornography and filtering programs for all household computers, etc.

The key here is to talk with your son; acknowledge his brand-new sexual appetite and the need he will have to look at girls, to want to touch them, and to be with them. Explain to him that he is normal, that there's nothing wrong with him. Tell him what it was like for you when you were his age, and how you were interested in the bodies of girls, the way they're built, their curves, soft hands, and pretty eyes.

Help your son to decide now *not* to have sexual intercourse with a girl until he's married. Tell him why waiting to save his body is so important, and why he will regret it if he doesn't. Warn him about the "sexual playground," and the many dangerous and often incurable sexually transmitted diseases, especially AIDS. Help him prepare a response to the old line, "If you loved me, you'd do it." Have him ready with the answer, "If you really loved me, you wouldn't ask!" Also, talk to him about not getting married too soon. Caution him that nearly half of all teenage marriages end in divorce. Help him to talk it through now, before he spends more and more time with someone of the opposite sex.

This is when he really needs you. You must become your son's primary source of information and guidance regarding sex. It's literally a matter of life or death! "Study after study demonstrates what many people know as common sense: parental involvement is the single most critical factor affecting the sexual activity of teens."[7]

Preparing Your Son for Marriage: The Context for Sexual Relations and a Whole Lot More

> If God meant woman to rule over man, He would have taken her out of Adam's head. Had He designed her to be his slave, He would have taken her out of his feet. But God took woman out of man's side, for He made her to be a helpmate and an equal to him.
>
> —Augustine

I remember an old song that goes, "I want a girl just like the girl that married dear ol' Dad." Those were the days! But the idea of marrying someone just like our mom or dad is not the stuff of legend and old wives' tales. And, in fact, research tells us that we are more likely to marry a person who resembles the parent with whom we have the most unresolved conflict. *Yikes!* Now that's a sobering thought.

Marriage is a risky enough proposition without dragging excess baggage from your past into it. Therefore, I strongly recommend that you connect or reconnect with your son right away and help him to enter into a right relationship with you. There is great truth to the axiom, "Marriage is not so much *finding* the right person as it is *being* the right person." When our sons enter into marriage as less than whole and happy people, they can be very needy and dependent, or aloof, resistant, and too independent. Their expectation can be, "My wife will give me love," and they may give little attention to their side of the agreement: "I will give love to my wife." And so, this emotional immaturity in marriage becomes one-sided and the goal becomes receiving, not giving.

Another may say, "My wife is there to do for me. I do my own thing, it's none of her business."

Lots of Christian men have a diseased mentality toward sexual identity and marriage!

The Bible teaches that in Christian marriage, the husband is to take the initiative in love; he is made responsible for the right kind of married love. In short, he is the lover. In Ephesians 5:25 the command is, "Husbands, love your wives." Dwight Harvey Small, in his book *Design for Christian Marriage,* says:

> Paul proceeds to set forth just exactly how husbands are to love their wives. It is "as Christ loved the church." Amazing! What loftier ideal could ever be put before husbands! The fullness of Christ's love for the church suggests five major characteristics for husbands to emulate by the power of the indwelling Holy Spirit:
>
> 1. Christ loved the church realistically. He was under no illusions when He sought us in love! It was not a romantic sentiment that moved the Son of God to love us. . . . Husbands, then, are to love their wives realistically. . . . It must embrace all of the faults and failures, the unlovely and disagreeable elements. For this Christ's love is adequate!
>
> 2. Christ loved the church sacrificially. He ". . . gave himself for her" (verse 25). How costly is love! . . . Husbands must love their wives sacrificially. They must be willing to give up all that is required to fulfill the life of the beloved. This may involve giving up some of their interests, their time, their pleasures, their ambitions, their friends. . . . Since it was a costly thing to accomplish redemption, and it is ever a costly thing to strive for holiness, the word [sacrifice] has come to mean "costliness in achieving some

end." How appropriate is this word, for marriage success is a costly thing, and the end is a holy end.

3. Christ loved the church purposefully. His purpose was "That he might present her to himself a glorious church . . . holy and without blemish" (verse 27). The purpose of Christ is the eventual perfection of His church. . . . In Christian marriage the husband is ever to seek a deepening unity with his beloved in thought, expression, and in the shared life. This he finds possible to accomplish through the Lord Jesus Christ, in whom the union is established and sustained.

4. Christ loved the church willfully. With no motivating cause outside himself, God willed to love us. . . . The mind, the heart and the will [of the husband] must cooperate in loving.

5. Finally, Christ loved the church absolutely. His love for us was without limit, without condition, and without reserve. . . . On the same principle all [the husband] does for his wife shall return in blessing upon himself.[8]

If I practice what I preach, my son will see a man who makes it his goal to balance sexuality with care, strength with compassion. He must bear witness to his mother returning love to me when I am realistic, sacrificial, purposeful, intentional, and faithful in my love for her. For my son to see this is to prepare him to achieve the kind of marriage every young Christian man dreams about.

Helping Your Son to Avoid the Myths of Marriage

There is so much more that needs to be said, but I would like to conclude this chapter with five myths of marriage our sons should be aware of before entering the marriage commitment. Some of these myths have been compiled by my friends Nick and Nancy Stinnet in their bestselling textbook *Relationships in Marriage and the Family.*[9]

Myth #1: Problems Galore. According to Nick and Nancy, the problems-galore myth says marriage and troubles are synonymous. As a result, people tend to view marriage very negatively. If they internalize the myth, people can marry expecting many problems. This, in turn, becomes the self-fulfilling prophecy in which we tend to consciously or subconsciously behave in a manner that brings about what we expected in the first place. They suggest that to achieve a rational and realistic approach to marriage, the positive as well as the negative aspects must be acknowledged.

Myth #2: Marriage Is a Downhill Experience. This myth, says the Stinnetts, maintains that as time passes, the marriage relationship becomes progressively less satisfying and exciting. Contrary to the downhill myth, social science research reports that many husbands and wives find the joy and contentment in their marriage increasing with time because the relationship has a chance to grow in depth and meaning.

Myth #3: Marriage Is a 50–50 Proposition. According to this myth, marriage is a 50–50 proposition, and with any disagreement or difficult situation, the husband and wife should meet each other halfway. The Stinnetts remind us, however, that most marital situations cannot be settled on a 50–50 basis. Relationships work better if each partner in a marriage is doing more than his or her "fair" share.

Myth #4: The Great Sex Difference. By stereotyping each other (e.g., women are more emotional than men, or men are better at abstract thinking, etc.), couples in a marriage end up relating more to the stereotypes than to each other. I recommend that we find out who we are as created in the image of God. Again, I suggest that you pick up a copy of the Penners' book *The Gift of Sex.*

Myth #5: The Successful Marriage Has No Conflict. Marriage therapists tell us that holding back a disappointment can actually harm a relationship. It's not conflict that's bad, it's how we handle it. We must teach our sons that conflict will be inevitable. The goal, therefore, is not to eliminate conflict but to manage it in a positive and effective manner. As someone has wisely discerned, "Attack the problem, not each other."

Helping Your Son Understand the Importance of Commitment

Of all the concepts to convey to your son, commitment needs to be on the top of the list. Dr. Nick Stinnett, in his pioneering research on family strengths, believes commitment is the key to a lasting marriage and high wellness among families. When I asked what commitment is in his estimation, Nick told me, "It's promoting the happiness and welfare of your wife and family over any other obligation by investing time with them. They simply come first." Then he offered the following suggestions for putting it to work:

1. Have a family council periodically, say, every six months. Ask, "How are we doing as a family? What needs to be changed?"
2. Some couples have discovered a heightened sense of commitment by renewing their marriage vows. A wedding anniversary is a good time to do this. Invite a few friends to witness the event and have an informal reception afterward. Your wife can wear her wedding dress or veil.
3. Rent a DVD that deals with commitment in relationships or good family life. *The War, Ordinary People,* and *The Blindside* are some examples. Watch your selection together, have popcorn, and then talk about what you have seen.
4. Trace your family tree. Public libraries and bookstores have materials on genealogy to help get you started. Sometimes genealogy classes are held at the YMCA, YWCA, or local community college.

Last but not least, I would add, have a devotional time as a couple. Commitment is derived from our relationship with God. The more we are committed to Him, the more we will be committed to each other.

Additional Resources

There are a number of resources to help you educate your son about sex.

First, there is the *Concordia Sex Education Series for Children* (St. Louis, MO: Concordia Publishing House, 1-800-325-3040). The books are written with specific age groups in mind. The information is in response to questions most typically asked by children. There is an emphasis on understanding sex as a God-given gift that is to be used responsibly. *Why Boys and Girls Are Different,* by Carol Greene, is for boys who are between the ages of three and five. *The Wonderful Way That Babies Are Made,* by Larry Christenson, is written for both younger and older boys and girls. *How You Are Changing,* by Jane Traver, is for ages eight through eleven. *Sex and the New You,* by Richard Bimler, is for ages eleven through fourteen. *Love, Sex, and God,* by Bill Ameiss and Jane Graver, is for ages fourteen and up. *How to Talk Confidently With Your Child About Sex,* by Lenore Buth, is a parent's guide for the whole series.

Some other books to consider are *How to Help Your Child Say No to Sexual Pressures,* by Josh McDowell; *How to Teach Your Child About Sex,* by my good friend Dr. Grace Ketterman; and *Preparing Youth for Dating, Courtship, and Marriage,* by Norman Wright. I'd also like to recommend that you get a copy of Josh McDowell's eight-part video series for parents of preteens and teens, entitled *How to Help Your Child Say No to Sexual Pressures.* This video is designed to help you as a father become more effective as the principal resource of sexual values to your son.

Here are some anti-pornography books, as well: *The Courage to Be Chaste* by Fr. Benedict Groeschel, CFR—a modern classic with many practical tips; *Boys to Men* by Tim Gray and Curtis Martin; *Theology of the Body for Beginners* by Christopher West; *Every Man's Battle, Every Young Man's Battle,* and *Preparing Your Son for Every Man's Battle* by Stephen Arterburn and Fred Stoeker; and *Breaking Free: 12 Steps to Sexual Purity* by Stephen Wood.

Christian websites:

- *www.pornharms.com*: A vast collection of peer-reviewed research on the harmfulness of pornography.
- *www.settingcaptivesfree.com*: A Christian website addressing many addictions, including pornography.
- *www.focusonthefamily.com*: A website that provides Christian resources for parenting.
- *www.freedomeveryday.org*: A site sponsored by L.I.F.E. Ministries (Living in Freedom Everyday), a sexual addiction recovery ministry.
- *www.thekingsmen.us*: The mission of this organization is, as men, to pledge to unite and build up other men in the mold of leader, protector, and provider through education, formation, and action.
- *http://somebodysdaughter.org*: A journey to freedom from pornography.
- *www.shelleylubben.net*: Shelley Lubben is an ex-porn star loving people out of porn. She's a wife and mother, ordained chaplain, and missionary to the sex industry, fighting for truth and an advocate for sex workers and porn performers who are abused by the adult industry.
- *www.thepinkcross.org/page/what-pink-cross*: "Where addicts get help and porn stars find hope." Founded by a former porn actress, this is a website for those trapped in the pornography industry or who want to see how UN-glamorous this lifestyle is.

For Thought and Discussion

1. How has your marital relationship affected your son's ideas of love, sex, and marriage?

2. How would your son describe your relationship to his mother?

3. What can you do to demonstrate to your son that you love him? Does he need to hear you say "I love you"? Does he need you to give him a hug?

4. What are some telltale signs that suggest your son might be struggling with pornography or being sexually active?

10

Behold My Beloved Son . . .

Presenting Your Son to the World

I never shall forget the joy
that suddenly was mine,
The sweetness of the thrill
that seemed to dance along my spine,
The pride that swelled within me
as he shook my youthful hand,
And treated me as big enough
with grown-up men to stand.
I felt my body straighten
and a stiffening at each knee,
And was gloriously happy,
just because he'd "mistered" me.

—From the poem
"Manhood's Greeting"[1]

Vertigo and smoke, carried on the haunting notes of flutes fashioned from hollowed bamboo shafts, floated into the Belly of the Crocodile. Eleven adolescent males sat cross-legged in a semicircle on the wooden floor, their wounds glistening as they listened intently to the music. No longer boys but not yet men, they were in the midst of the manhood ritual of scarification, a month-long physical and mental ordeal designed to enlighten them with knowledge and courage, but also burden them with the responsibility of being men in the remote Papua New Guinea village of Kanganaman. Scars inflicted during the ceremony run the length of their bodies, resembling wounds left by the teeth of a crocodile during an attack. The effect is to make them men, with row after row of scalelike raised flesh, to resemble the reptile they both fear and revere.

Watbangu, a twenty-year-old initiate, leaned close and spoke in a low voice. The flutes were singing the *Song of the Crocodile,* he explained, signifying the joy the elders felt because the boys were becoming men. To the boys' biological mothers, the music symbolized the loss of sons who would no longer answer to women—mothers or otherwise. "Sometimes when our mothers hear the music, they cry," Watbangu whispered through the haze of three smoldering fires.[2]

I'm not into pagan ritual, but there is something deep within men that longs to know they are accepted into the realm of manhood. That they are considered by other men to be capable, strong, *male.*

It is my belief that we, as fathers, need to make a time and place to signal the passage into manhood for our sons, and to do so from a uniquely Christian perspective. Before we present them to the world, we can help our sons make the transition that says to them, "You are no longer a boy, but a young man."

Helping them make this transition will not be as easy as you think. This move away from boyhood toward manhood may be very subtle at first—so keep your eyes open! Perhaps the best indicator will come from your wife, who, like the mothers in our story above, will begin to feel the loss of her son. My friend John Smith tells a wonderful yet painful story of his mother's reluctance to let him grow up.

> I was a freshman in high school trying out for the football team. My coach had given me a parental permission form that my mother and father had to sign in order for me to play, and a form to be filled out by a doctor which said that I was healthy enough to be kicked, knocked down, beaten and pounded mercilessly with no permanent damage to my body. . . .
>
> Well, the worst possible thing happened in practice that afternoon. We were running a simple tackling drill, which was designed to teach us how to knock the ball loose from the runner by using our helmets. Somehow, I caught my cheekbone on the shoulder pad of the runner I was tackling. The collision removed a patch of skin about the size of a silver dollar. It wasn't serious, but the red, raw, exposed flesh looked terrible.
>
> My mother was working and didn't get home until 5:30 or 6:00, so it had been pretty easy to disguise my whereabouts after school. Of course when I got home, she was there and it all came out. I had the forms in my hand and my speech ready, but I didn't get to give it.
>
> "What happened to your face?" she asked, a certain urgency in her voice.

"I was playing football with some guys after school," I hedged.

"How many times have I told you not to play that game? It's too rough."

"Several times." I didn't mention the forms. I went to my room and waited for my dad to get home.

After supper I took the parental consent form to him and explained that I needed his signature. Although my facial laceration had been quite a topic at the table, he took the form, told me to get a pen and he signed it.

"I have to have mom's signature too," I explained.

"Sure," he said, "take it to her and tell her I said to sign it."

I took it into the kitchen, explained briefly, and showed her where to sign. She got real upset and said she wasn't going to do any such thing—I must be crazy to have asked her. I showed her where dad had signed and told her he said that she should sign too.

"Well, you can tell him that he must be crazy too."

I went back into the living room. "She won't sign it," I told him.

He put the paper down. "Did you tell her I said to?"

"Yes."

"What did she say?"

"She said that you must be crazy."

"Let me have that form."

He took the card and went into the kitchen. I followed, heart in my mouth. . . . My dad walked over, put his hands on Mom's shoulders and said, "Florence, it's for the best. He's got to have a chance to prove himself."

"Oh, you men," she said. I didn't understand it then, and only understand a little of it now—but you wives and mothers out there know what "Oh, you men" means.

She dried her eyes on her apron and sat down at the cardboard card table that was our kitchen table. She took the form from my dad and began to read it. There were several clauses and questions—who to contact in case of injury, what medications was I allergic to, the name of our family doctor, and if hospitalization was required what facility was I to be taken to—stuff that would make any person apprehensive. She picked up the pen, and started to cry. I thought she had changed her mind, but she signed it. She looked up at me and said, "Go on, play football. Knock your teeth loose and break your nose—for what? Well, I don't have to watch, and I won't." Then she put her face in her hands and she really cried. . . . [3]

So how did you know when you had passed the "test" and moved from boyhood to manhood? Was it parental consent to join the football team? Was it when you got your driver's license? When you graduated from high school? College? Maybe when you were old enough to vote. Let's face it. Many of us struggled to know when . . . and perhaps from time to time still struggle. Does being married with kids make you a man? If not, then what does?

It's interesting to me that Paul, in his first letter to the Corinthians, writes about manhood. It's only one verse, really, but taken in context it may help shed light on this confusing subject. "When I was a child, I talked like a child, I thought like a child, I reasoned like a child. When I became a man, I put childish ways behind me" (13:11). What were these "childish ways"? Well, a careful reading of Paul's letter identifies several immature practices:

- an inability to get along with others (1:10; 4:21)

- immorality (5; 6:12–20)
- litigation in pagan courts (6:1–8)

To be childish, according to Paul, was to be a part of jealousy and envy, to use vulgar language, to be involved in power struggles, to be guilty of verbal or physical abuse of your wife, to have ungoverned sexual fantasies, to be guilty of drug abuse or alcohol addiction, to use your God-given gifts and natural talents for self-aggrandizement.

The bottom line was that the Corinthians had a problem in Christian conduct. They had right beliefs, but they had failed to continue to develop character in relationship to their bodies, to God, and to others. In other words, they professed belief in Jesus, but they didn't act like Him. To be strong, loving, self-controlled, as was Christ, is the hallmark of Christian maturity. It is the sum total of what it means to be a man.

Conversely, to be self-centered, demanding, or abusive—in word or conduct—is to remain a child, though in a man's body. It's the Peter Pan syndrome, when men can't love or be loving and are trapped in perpetual adolescence. They become focused on themselves and not on their wives and children.

Consider this: *When a man can't love, he can't lead.*

We must ask of our son, "How loving is he?" Is he getting the message that real men are patient, kind, not envious, not boastful, not proud, not rude, not self-seeking, not easily angered, not unforgiving, not delighting in evil, rejoicing in truth, protecting, trusting, hoping, persevering, and never failing in love (see 1 Corinthians 13:4–8)?

When these fruits of God's Spirit are manifest in ever-increasing degrees, then at a point determined by both his father and mother, a son is ready to enter manhood. Only then should he be permitted to stand in the company of men and enter into covenant love with God and his neighbor (see Matthew 22:34–40).

Timid Timothy and Powerful Paul

A biblical example of a person struggling to grow up is Timothy. Timothy was in training under the apostle Paul to be a leader of the church in Ephesus. There was only one problem: Timothy had a "spirit of timidity." Apparently this lack of confidence was a serious obstacle for him (2 Timothy 1:7). So much so that Paul had to write to Timothy in an earlier letter, "Don't let anyone look down on you because you are young . . ." (1 Timothy 4:12). Timothy was probably in his mid-thirties or younger, and in that day, such an influential position was not usually held by a man so young and so obviously lacking in confidence. Perhaps for this reason, the older men were questioning his authority.

Timothy was a man who received his religious instruction and knowledge of God through his maternal lineage: his grandmother, Lois, and his mother, Eunice (2 Timothy 1:5). From childhood he had been taught the Old Testament. But because his father was a Greek and not a Jew, Timothy would not have been equipped to know much about manhood in a Jewish community. Even Paul anticipated this liability and circumcised him (Acts 16:3).

Later, Paul ordained Timothy by laying hands on him (2 Timothy 1:6). He also had the elders at Ephesus lay their hands on him (1 Timothy 4:14). These three acts—circumcision, ordination, and laying on of hands by the elders—are a kind of "rite of passage" for Timothy. We have no clue as to whether he had otherwise been instructed on the virtues, responsibilities, and expectations of manhood. Maybe a lack of preparation by his father caused Timothy to be insecure in his role as a leader. Could this be why Paul "adopted" Timothy as his spiritual son, becoming his surrogate father and mentor in the faith? (1 Timothy 1:2, 18; 2 Timothy 1:2; 2:1).

Paul's instructions to Timothy often sound like a father's instruction to his son—to enable him, to empower him, and to pass on to him the mantle of manhood. This becomes more obvious in 2 Timothy 2:22, when Paul tells him: "Flee the evil desires of youth, and pursue righteousness, faith, love and peace, along with those who call on the Lord out of a pure heart." In 1 Corinthians 13:11, Paul uses somewhat similar language, as we have already seen, to talk about young faith versus mature faith: "When I was a child, I talked like a child, I thought like a child, I reasoned like a child. When I became a man, I put childish ways behind me."

By adopting Timothy as his son, instructing him, and providing him a "rite of passage" before presenting him to the world, Paul called him to manhood—to accept the full measure of his uniqueness as a man, something Timothy's grandmother and mother, for all their good intentions, apparently could not do.

Conferring on Your Son a Sense of Manhood

Blake's father, Kent, and I were in a group that met regularly for more than three years for prayer, confession, and personal accountability. Kent knew it was time to bring his son into the company of other men. Blake's baptism would take place the following day, but tonight he would leave his mother and all that was genteel and safe and join his father's friends.

Blake was visibly nervous. He didn't know what to expect as his father picked him up from the house and drove him to an agreed-upon site to meet the others. "What's going on?" asked Blake, breaking the silence. "Am I in trouble?"

"No, no," his father assured him. "Just sit back, son, and relax. You have a job to do, and I'm going to help you do it. No more questions."

Kent pulled up to where the other men, including myself, were waiting. We all got into the car, sandwiching Blake between us. I could see his anxiety, sense his tension. We smiled at each other. I knew it would be a night he'd never forget.

It was decided beforehand that we would take Blake to an authentic western ranch steak restaurant just outside of town. We feasted on rib-eyes and baked potatoes.

Blake took in every sight, every sound. He was attentive to every slap on the back, every story told, every joke shared. He was sitting with men he knew his father greatly admired, men he had seen before studying God's Word, on their knees in prayer. That night, the smile on his face showed that he felt as if he belonged.

After dinner, we drove to a nearby state park.

We all climbed out of the car, each of us carrying something under our arms. We walked for about a half hour into the most remote part of the park. Finally we came upon a clearing and sat down in a circle surrounded by trees. A cool breeze swept through the foliage, creating an almost eerie feeling. A Thermos was brought out and cups distributed. We all toasted the evening with our coffee, to the glory of God. Then Blake's father spoke.

"My son," Kent began. "I've longed for this night almost as much as I longed for your birth. Your mother and I prayed for a child to call our own. It wasn't easy, as you know. Mom lost many babies before you were born. We wept and pleaded with God to give us just one child. And He gave us you. Now, tonight, because you have decided to be baptized tomorrow, I have brought you out to be with my best friends—to help you in your passage to becoming a young man. I want you to know that your mother and I are very, very proud of you. We love you, Blake."

Father and son hugged and wept together as the men sang a blessing over them: "We Love You With the Love of the Lord." Each man in turn told Blake what they thought was the meaning of manhood, and then gave him a token of their esteem and affection.

Then it was my turn.

I took out my army dress uniform, with its chaplain crosses on the lapels and the lieutenant bars on the epaulets. I told Blake, in brief, that joining the army didn't make me a man. Jesus Christ did. I then gave him one of the crosses from my uniform. Pinning it onto his shirt collar, I could see that he was moved. I was, too. When we left for home, Blake asked, "Michael, may I please carry your uniform to the car?"

There was silence as we drove home. Blake, no longer a boy but not yet a man, was quiet—no doubt thinking about the significance of the night's events.

At his baptism the next day, I was pleased to see the chaplain's cross still pinned to his collar. His father presented him to the brothers and sisters who had come as witnesses. His mother, Kim, helped to prepare him for the plunge, and then Blake straightened up tall as his father lowered him beneath the water. He went under a boy; he came out a young man.

For you and your son, it will be a different story. Maybe you will lead him to the brink of manhood the weekend you take him on his first backpacking trip into the wilderness. Maybe it will be the period of time when you help him choose a college and prepare him to leave home, or when you help him learn responsibility by owning his first car. Maybe when you prepare him for the challenges he will face joining the army. The idea is to send your son out into the world with a sense that *Dad believes I'm capable and resourceful enough to manage myself. He believes I can stay out of trouble—or get myself out of it! And he respects me enough to include me in his circle of peers.*

Letting My Son Go

It was the day I'd been waiting for; perhaps, even dreading. My son was leaving home. It was time for him to put God's Word and principles to use, hammering them out on the anvil of life where he would work, marry, have children of his own, and grow old. I would bear my grief in silence. I knew the perils of the world that awaited him, but his time had come. I had to let him go.

He was anxious to get out on his own. He had packed his belongings, loaded them up in the car, and he was ready to leave. I held him, but only for a moment. He broke my paternal grasp. We smiled at each other. And waving good-bye, he drove away. I watched as the distance between me and that old car grew. I wanted to run down the driveway after him. I wanted to shout, "Don't go, son! Please, don't go!"

Of course, I didn't.

That day felt like forever.

I was releasing my son to learn from life's hard knocks. Yet I knew that because I reared my son by God's standards and by my good example, he'd do just fine. I trusted him. More important, I trusted God—to whom I now address this prayer, adapted from Proverbs 3:1–4:

Oh, Lord, may my son never forget your teaching. Let his heart keep your commandments. Then, Lord, you will give many more days and years to his life and you will add your peace.

May kindness and truth never leave him, Lord. May he bind them around his neck and write them on his heart.

Then, Lord, you will give him favor and a good reputation both with you and with man.

For Thought and Discussion

1. How does the imagery of a caterpillar emerging from its cocoon as a butterfly apply to the task of preparing your son for life?

2. What everyday object could you use as a word picture to praise your son, or what God-given gift could you point to in his life that could be used in the future?

3. How did you know when you were a man? What was your rite of passage? Did your father participate in it?

Notes

Chapter 1: Before Your Son Faces the World

1. Jeff Giles, "The Music Man, the Family Man," *Newsweek*, October 23, 1995, 72.

2. David Simmons, *Dad the Family Coach* (Wheaton, IL: Victor Books, 1991), 40.

Chapter 2: Effective Fathering

1. Frank Clancy, "Breaking Away: What Happens When a Son Determines to Live a Life in Opposition to His Father?" *Los Angeles Times Magazine*, June 21, 1992, 20.

2. Ibid.

3. Thomas Lickona, *Raising Good Children* (New York: Bantam Books, 1983), 22.

4. Tory Hayden, "Conversations Kids Crave," *Families*, June 1982.

5. Andrew Murray, *Like Christ* (Springdale, PA: Whitaker House, 1983).

Chapter 3: What's Happening to My Son?

1. Erik Erikson, *Childhood and Society*, 2nd edition (New York: Norton, 1963).

2. Thomas Gordon, *Parent Effectiveness Training* (New York: Wyden, 1970).

3. Thomas Lickona, 271.

Chapter 4: The Bird That Gets the Worm: Preparing Your Son to Work

1. Paul and Sarah Edwards, *Making It On Your Own* (New York: The Putnam Publishing Group, 1991), 120.

2. A.C. Green, *Victory* (Lake Mary, FL: Creation House, 1994), 64–65.

3. Stephen Covey, *The Seven Habits of Highly Effective People* (New York: Simon & Schuster, 1990), 174–176.

4. Ibid., 202.

Chapter 5: "All Work and No Play . . ." Helping Your Son to Enjoy Life

1. Walter Wangerin Jr., "Hans Christian Andersen: Shaping the Child's Universe," *Reality and the Vision* (Waco, TX: Word Publishers, 1990), 1.

2. Esther Forbes.

3. Stephen Crane.

4. Jack London.

5. Ruth Stafford Peale, *Secrets of Staying in Love* (Nashville, TN: Thomas Nelson, 1984), 404.

6. Tim Hansel, *Creative Fathering* (Tarrytown, NY: Revell), 21.

7. Mike Yorkey and Greg Johnson, *Daddy's Home* (Colorado Springs, CO: Focus on the Family, 1992), 14–15.

Chapter 6: Seek Ye First the Kingdom of God: Helping Your Son to Be a Disciple of Christ

1. Richard Foster, *Celebration of Discipline* (New York: Harper & Row, 1978), 7.

2. Andrew Murray, *How to Raise Your Children for Christ* (Minneapolis, MN: Bethany House Publishers, 1975), 12.

3. *Disciple's Study Bible,* New International Version, "Life Helps" section, Zondervan.

4. Richard Foster, *Celebration of Discipline,* 148.

5. Michael O'Donnell, *Home from Oz* (Dallas, TX: Word Publishers, 1994), 181.

Chapter 7: Bad Company Corrupts Good Morals: Helping Your Son to Choose the Right Friends

1. Everett Shostrom, *Man, the Manipulator* (New York: Abingdon Press, 1967).

Chapter 8: "Ask Not What Your Country Can Do for You . . ." Helping Your Son to Be a Good Citizen

1. Carl F.H. Henry, *Aspects of Christian Social Ethics* (Grand Rapids, MI: Eerdmans Publishing Co., 1964).

2. John R. Stott, *God's New Society: The Message of Ephesians* (Downers Grove, IL: InterVarsity Press, 1980).

Chapter 9: The Birds and the Bees: Helping Your Son to Understand His Sexuality and to Prepare for Marriage

1. Schwarzbeck, "Children Today," *Abilene Reporter News,* January 13, 1992.

2. Cited in the film *Productivity and Self-Fulfilling Prophecy: The Pygmalion Effect* (Carlsbad, CA: CRM Productions, 1987).

3. Gary Smalley and John Trent, *The Blessing* (Nashville, TN: Thomas Nelson, 1986).

4. Clifford and Joyce Penner, *The Gift of Sex* (Dallas, TX: Word Publishers, 1983), 29.

5. Gordon Dalbey, "Beyond Fig Leaves and Cooties: Loving a Woman," *The Making of a Marriage* (Nashville, TN: Thomas Nelson, 1993), 23.

6. James Dobson, *Preparing for Adolescence* (Santa Ana, CA: Vision House Publishers, 1978), 87.

7. Jim Whitmer, *How to Help Your Kids Say No to Sex* (Colorado Springs: Focus on the Family, 1993), 5.

8. Dwight H. Small, *Design for Christian Marriage* (Old Tappan, NJ: Spire Books, 1974), 86–90.

9. Nick and Nancy Stinnett, *Relationships in Marriage and the Family* (Old Tappan, NJ: Macmillan, 1991), 56–62.

Chapter 10: Behold My Beloved Son . . . Presenting Your Son to the World

1. Edgar A. Guest, *Just Folks* (Chicago, IL: The Reilly & Lee Co., 1917).

2. Taken from "In the Belly of the Crocodile," *American Way* (February 1, 1992), 53.

3. John Smith, *My Mother Played the Piano* (Nashville, TN: Twentieth-Century Christian, 1993), 25–28.

Michael A. O'Donnell graduated with a PhD from Kansas State University and is best known for his National Adolescent Wellness Research Project, co-conducted with family strengths scholar Professor Nick Stinnett, PhD. Their research has been the focus of numerous books, radio, TV, and print features, such as *USA Today*, *Better Homes and Gardens*, and *Ebony-Jet* magazines, as well as CNN Evening News, Associated Press, CBS Interactive Business Network, and ABC's nationally syndicated radio program, *The Best of Our Knowledge*. Dr. O'Donnell has an active blog and speaking ministry and lives with his wife, Rachel, in Ogdensburg, New York, where he also serves as the senior pastor for St. John's Church.